Start-up CEO's Marketing Manual

Guy Smith

Free Thinkers Media

2360 Corporate Circle · Suite 400
Henderson, NV 89074

DEDICATION

To Calvin Fowler, my first boss after leaving college. He had the patience of a saint (which I still lack) and a keen focus on core issues (which I developed under his tutelage). To say Cal was formative in my business life is akin to saying oxygen is valuable.

CONTENTS

Foreword and Forewarned

Nobody in Silicon Valley ever starved because they lacked innovation.

Management guru and thought leader Peter Drucker once said that business has only two functions – innovation and marketing. Everything else is administrative work.

You are reading this book because you have come to the uncomfortable realization that the innovations you want to unleash upon the world go nowhere unless they are marketed ... and that you don't know marketing.

As a founder or CEO, you don't need to know every excruciating detail about marketing. Enjoy the bliss that ignorance about multivariate in-page search optimization brings. Waste not a moment on why the 47th shade of blue is not a good match for your brand. Though essential, these details are handled by marketing practitioners who as a class are relatively cheap. But they cannot do their job unless a sound strategy for going to market has been devised, written, published and monitored. You, the business leader, must assure that your marketing strategy covers all bases and sets a foundation for others to succeed.

And you don't know marketing strategy.

Your goal is to understand marketing strategy at a very high level. This assures that you complete your go-to-market plan, that you have a realistic idea of how you will succeed and that your first marketing hires don't drive your company into bankruptcy by driving your products into marketing black holes. The discipline of marketing strategy clarifies, classifies and debunks wishful and fuzzy thinking. It is knowing, as opposed to guessing. It is a battle plan that George Patton would have envied.

This book is your introduction to every element of marketing strategy. With it you have a checklist of topics, one that you should literally check off as each subject is investigated and documented. If you are just conceptualizing your product, it can keep you from developing something that never sells. If you are seeking investors, it keeps you from being rejected for having an incomplete go-to-market plan. If you are in a highly competitive situation, you will learn how to skip past, circle and strangle your competition. It is the catapult that launches your product instead of letting it sink into the market mire.

Start-up CEO's Marketing Manual is admittedly focused on high technology products with a bit of bias toward business-to-business (B2B) offerings. Don't let this perspective – a byproduct of my quarter century of experience – distract you. The lessons here apply to nearly every market, every category and every product. But if you head an organization, or work in the marketing department of one that vends technology products, consider yourself lucky. Start-up CEO's Marketing Manual will resonate perfectly with you, providing the same degree of insight and satisfaction your competitors will soon lack.

Unless they are reading Start-up CEO's Marketing Manual too.

Chapter 1 – Marketing Strategy Layers

What is marketing?

Seriously. Before reading another word, put down this book and grab your iPad. Fire up Notes and jot down a one or two sentence definition of marketing. When done, come back to me and let's discuss marketing at the conceptual level.

I had you write down your definition of marketing because there is a lot of confusion among founders (especially techie founders) as to what marketing is and how it works. If what you authored is significantly off base from the following discussion, then you bought this book just in time.

The concise definition of marketing is:

The strategy and tactics for creating and promoting products that people want to buy.

That sounds simple, but in practice it is very complicated and much more scientific than most folks think. Let's break down and examine the definition so you get a full frontal view of what you face as a corporate leader.

Strategy and tactics: This is where most people fall off the conceptual boat. To many folks, marketing is equated with promotions, and promotions are incorrectly equated with being purely tactical activities. Great products require both – a strategy for developing and promoting a product. Strategy development has a series of tactical activities, but these are separate from promotional activities.

Creating and promoting: Core to marketing strategy is the creation of the product. Many products, especially in Silicon Valley, are created in near information vacuums – conceptualized and built on vague speculations and observations about some perceived need. This is not bad in and of itself, but more often than not ...

That people want to buy: ... vague market insights create products that few people want. Often it is not enough to create a good product. You have to create desire for the product you have. Apple sold iPods not by listing audio fidelity specs, but by using happy, dancing silhouettes to associate the joy of music to Apple gizmos.

What is marketing?

- It is the strategy and tactics for creating and promoting products that people want to buy
- Inbound marketing
  - Gathering information that defines markets and products
- Outbound marketing
  - Communicating to people about your products

Given this definition, two divisions rapidly appear: inbound and outbound marketing. [1] Inbound marketing refers to the inflow of information that define the product and to help refine promotional strategy. Outbound are the strategies and tactics used in communicating to

---

[1] The phrases "inbound" and "outbound" have recently been corrupted by youngsters. Herein we use the traditional definitions.

your customers. Inbound marketing is nearly all strategy and outbound is largely tactical, and yes the two overlap a bit. Yet it is wise to compartmentalize these to improve your organization and keep your sanity.

Inbound marketing is the gathering of information that helps to define both your market and your product. Inbound marketing can be as complex as statistically detailed surveys of buying patterns, competitor feature lists, gap analysis, and multi-dimensional segmentation studies. It can also be as simple as listening to your customers. Inbound marketing is the most underused marketing discipline and yet it is the most critical. It is also uniquely found in the strategic marketing arena.

Outbound marketing is communicating to interested parties about your product and your company. These people are primarily buyers, but you also communicate to analysts, reporters, shareholders, and if you are really good, to your competitors. Nothing spooks a competitor as thoroughly as communicating to them, and in ways that show you play the game of marketing chess better than they.

Now that you have a working idea of what marketing is, let's expose what marketing is not.

What marketing is *not*

- ## Marketing is not sales
  - Sales is an intelligent, responsive, real-time communications device
- ## Marketing is not advertising
  - Advertising is one very small (and shrinking) part of outbound communications
- ## Marketing is not mere promotions
  - Marketing is a cradle-to-grave, perpetual, 360° set of integrated processes

---

Marketing is not sales: Sales implements small parts of outbound marketing. It is an intelligent, real-time communications mechanism and is indispensable. But it has nothing to do with the science of marketing.

Marketing is not advertising: Like sales, advertising is a means to communicate your marketing decisions.

Marketing is not promotions: If fact, any kind of promotion — sales, advertising, web banners, buzz — are subsets of marketing and generally outbound and tactical in nature. They apply, but they are tactical activities and not marketing per se.

Marketing is a 360 degree, perpetual, cradle-to-grave set of integrated processes. Sales, advertising and other promotions are part of the total process, but only a part and frankly the part that fail if the other parts – the strategic aspects – are not executed correctly.

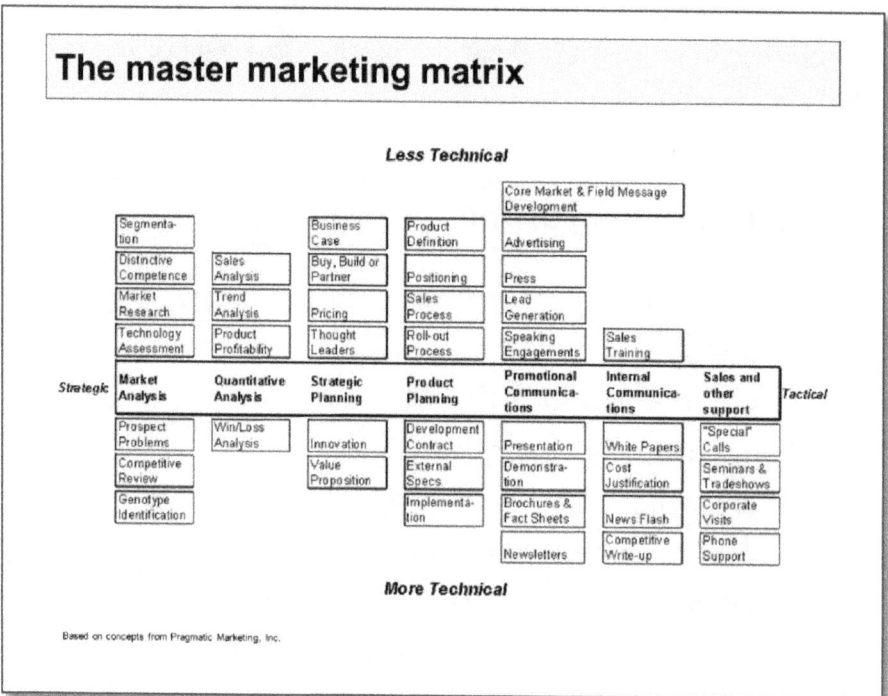

The master marketing matrix

Less Technical

					Core Market & Field Message Development		
	Segmentation		Business Case	Product Definition	Advertising		
	Distinctive Competence	Sales Analysis	Buy, Build or Partner	Positioning	Press		
	Market Research	Trend Analysis	Pricing	Sales Process	Lead Generation		
	Technology Assessment	Product Profitability	Thought Leaders	Roll-out Process	Speaking Engagements	Sales Training	
Strategic	**Market Analysis**	**Quantitative Analysis**	**Strategic Planning**	**Product Planning**	**Promotional Communications**	**Internal Communications**	**Sales and other support**	*Tactical*
	Prospect Problems	Win/Loss Analysis	Innovation	Development Contract	Presentation	White Papers	"Special" Calls
	Competitive Review		Value Proposition	External Specs	Demonstration	Cost Justification	Seminars & Tradeshows
	Genotype Identification			Implementation	Brochures & Fact Sheets	News Flash	Corporate Visits
					Newsletters	Competitive Write-up	Phone Support

More Technical

Based on concepts from Pragmatic Marketing, Inc.

I augmented this chart originally from Pragmatic Marketing. All the buckets on this chart are marketing functions. On the left are strategic tasks and on the right are tactical ones. What becomes clear is that performing anything on the right side of this chart without first completing all, or at least most, of the buckets on the left is a mistake. For example, sending a salesman on calls without composing his marketing messages or identifying target buyer profiles would be wasted effort.

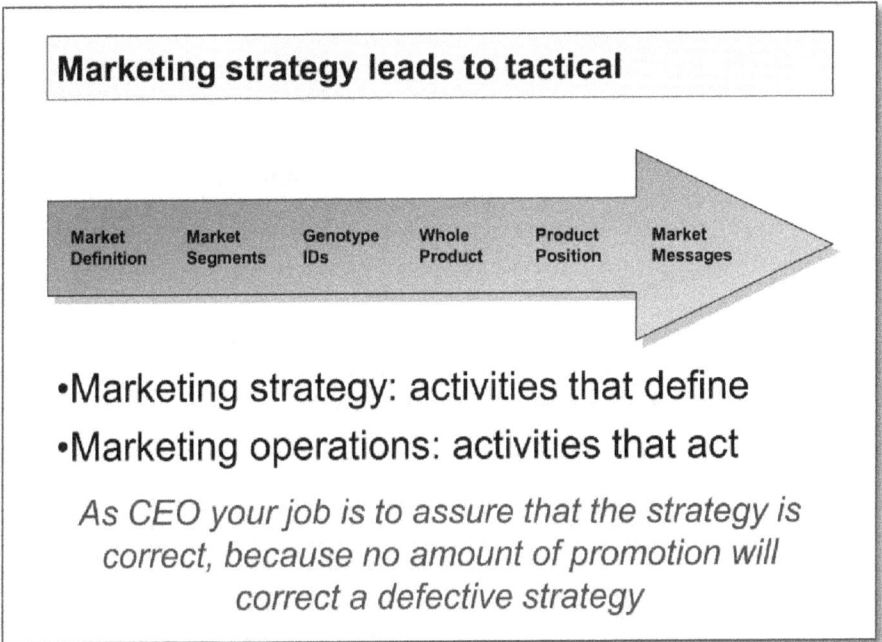

Marketing strategy leads to tactical

Market Definition	Market Segments	Genotype IDs	Whole Product	Product Position	Market Messages

- Marketing strategy: activities that define
- Marketing operations: activities that act

As CEO your job is to assure that the strategy is correct, because no amount of promotion will correct a defective strategy

This chart (available in a more usable form by contacting Silicon Strategies Marketing) is your top-level check list. If you and your team cannot mark most of the boxes as completed in the first four columns, then you do not have a go-to-market strategy. A simpler arrow diagram shows the major strategic marketing functions to which you must attend. Just remember two immutable laws: strategy defines tactical operations and you are responsible for strategy. Even if you hire a good director or VP of marketing, you are still responsible to make sure they complete the marketing strategy checklist and have your company ready to compete.

And here is a million-dollar management secret: marketing strategy defines what you as a company will do. When the marketing is well thought out, based on good information, and clearly communicated, then marketing operations are nearly self-executing. Otherwise, chaos follows. Marketing without sound strategy is like driving cross-country without a roadmap. Sure, you will get somewhere, just not where you want to be. Your job is to assure that your marketing strategy is correct. No amount of promotions or operational efficiency will compensate for a bad strategy.

Marketing strategy is composed of layers. These layers are like mathematics. You cannot hope to understand calculus if you have not learned algebra, and you cannot learn algebra if you have not mastered arithmetic. When you approach your product launch, start at the bottom of the stack and work your way up. Sadly, many tech founders start at *positioning* and then wonder why they cannot get market traction.

The seven essential elements of marketing strategy, in order from the most fundamental upward are:

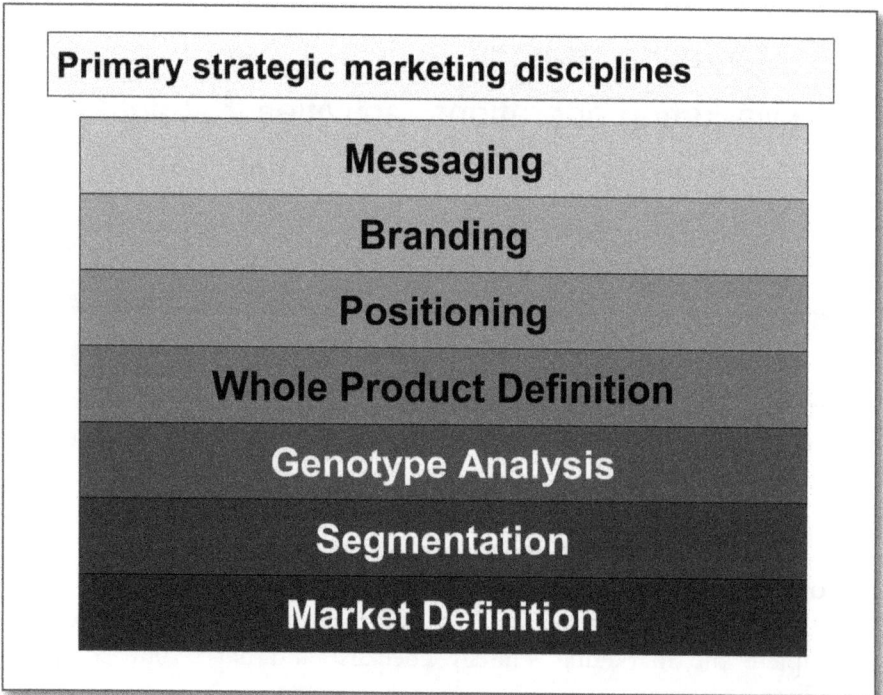

Primary strategic marketing disciplines
Messaging
Branding
Positioning
Whole Product Definition
Genotype Analysis
Segmentation
Market Definition

Market definition: Understanding the physics of your market. This exposes the scope and competitive landscape of your market. If you are seeking investment capital and have not done a good job of defining your market, you will remain unfunded. As one who has sat on the investor side of pitch sessions, I can say with certainty that this is one of the red flags over which investors will not take you seriously.

Segmentation: The process of dividing your market into small, addressable and prioritized submarkets. You cannot determine how best to segment your market if you do not understand the size, scope and competitive landscape of your market. And you must segment your market because you cannot possibly sell to your entire potential market (not even IBM can).

Genotypes:[2] The people who make or influence the decision to buy your products. You must understand their motivations to buy, and these motivations are typically different from segment to segment and from genotype to genotype. They are also rational and emotional.

Whole Product Definition: The complete set of expected outcomes a customer wants. This set of expected and desired outcomes helps you to create the best possible product and find the best combination of building, buying, or partnering.

Positioning: Determining and adjusting where in the market your product sits compared to alternatives. When people refer to positioning they could be talking about either the determination of your actual position or the promotion of the position you want people to believe your product has (and the two better not be too far apart or you will destroy your brand and future).

Branding: Making the market think and feel what *you* want them to about your product. If you do not clearly define your brand, you cannot communicate it, and if you cannot communicate it nobody will know or care what you sell.

Messaging: The construction of words, images, videos or any other content that attracts target genotypes in prioritized segments to your Whole Product. Every stage before messaging – market definition through branding – contributes to your messaging, and messaging is your last step before reaching out to buyers.

Let's start digging into the details.

---

[2] These are also known as "personae" and the terms are nearly interchangeable.

Market Definition

Market definition is the beginning of the process whereby you seek to understand the metrics of your market on the macro level. Some start-ups do a poor job of scoping their markets and tell themselves many lies about the market they want to serve. The moment they tell these lies to an investor, the investor invites them to leave.

Market definition – why do it?

- Understand the market size and potential
  - Total market
  - Addressable market
  - Realistic market
- Understand the competitive *issues*
- Identify trends (direction) in the market
- Map the geographic realities of the market
- Seek commonalities of market disciplines of buyers (B2B)
- Determine markets' channel opportunities and realities
- Estimate market penetration realities
- It is *not* to validate your preconceptions about your product

---

To understand market definition, you have to understand that there are three different levels of market scope you need to measure:

Total market: This is the number of buyers who *could* be potential customers. In theory, everybody is a potential customer for rubber bands. But how many elastic rings do you find in Sentinelese villages? The next subset is …

Addressable market: Your addressable market is the number of buyers who are candidates for your product as it exists (or will exist once you finish building it). Once you subtract from the total market those people who cannot afford your product, for who critical features are lacking, and who are prohibited by law from obtaining your product, or who display some other limiting factor, you derive your addressable market.

Realistic market: Your realistic market are the number of buyers in your addressable market that you can realistically reach given time, budget and manpower constraints. As a quick aside, these are not all of the factors to weigh when defining your realistic market.

You will also need to scope:

Competitive issues: This includes not only competing products, but alternate commercial solutions, open source solutions, home grown alternatives, and of course competing against the way customers are handling their problems now.

Trends: A lot of money has been thrown away by ignoring trends and selling against a tide. Sun Micro was famous for this.

Geography: Mainly economic geography, but any restrictions and barriers to entry into certain markets. If you try selling SARBOX compliance software into Nigeria you will find that geography paired with the lacking need for compliance creates few buyers.

Market disciplines: You need to study the market disciplines of your target customers to identify commonalities. Understanding if your product amplifies only one of the common market disciplines will reduce your addressable market size.

Channels: A rational review of channels will help determine your realistic market. In almost all cases, you cannot sell to everyone yourself. If channels do not exist, you will have to adjust your go-to-market plan accordingly.

This all leads to making *realistic* assumptions about your market, *not* validating your preconceptions. More start-ups have failed or not received investor cash because their go-to-market plans were based on pie-in-the-sky hopes and not restrained goals based on clear understanding of the market and market/product limitations. You can fool yourself all you like, but angels and VCs are not fooled at all.

Let's explore the three market sizing's and related topics in more detail.

The **total market** is the total number of purchases made by every conceivable consumer of your product, plus rational estimates on growth rates. Analyst groups often have quality data on total markets, but they often do not size your specific market or new markets that you may be pioneering.

This is a serious problem for start-ups. It is nice to have hard data, but if you are truly innovating – creating something that doesn't exist or is a vast improvement upon current offerings – then hard data about your markets may not exist within the bowels of your favorite analyst group. This problem is not unsolvable. Two solid methods for at least extrapolating market size estimates include:

Find similar markets or ones populated by similar customers, and estimate your market potential from there (e.g., proxy browser nanny filters using consumer installations of anti-virus software)

Build estimates from the ground up using demographic buyer profiles and complimentary data (add census data to the example above to find targetable households).

Market definition elements – market sizes

- Total market
  - All potential sales of a whole product
  - Estimate growth rates
- Addressable market
  - Market share that can conceivably be won with the current product
- Realistic (sellable) market
  - What part of the market can you actually sell to, given operational and competitive issues
- Market geographies
  - Realistic market less non-valuable regions
- Metrics
  - Revenues
  - Units
  - Support/subscription revenues

As noted above, the **addressable market** is the subset of the total market that you can actually reach. Apple's iPods are a good example. The total market for iPods is every human who likes listening to music, which is close to every human on the planet. Apple's addressable market excludes tribal members squatting in huts in New Guinea, people without computers to download music from, and extraterrestrials without ears who listen to music telepathically.

Your **realistic or sellable market** is a subset of your addressable market bounded by other constraining factors. Let's say you make a widget that works on original model iPods but not the current model. Your realistic market is at best a subset of the iPod market. More importantly, dynamic market factors – such as your product not being localized for foreign markets – are constrains that define your realistic market.

Here is a harsh reality. Investors, angels and VCs, understand realistic market. I have seen VCs ask one pointed question to test if founders were pitching total, addressable or realistic markets (and the VC's became instantly disinterested if the answers were not the latter). If you do not have a reasonable grasp of what your realistic market is today and in the next planned position within the market, investors will tell you to finish your homework ... if they bother talking to you at all.

When assembling your market size estimates, triangulate between various price points, low/realistic/high unit penetration, and recurring revenue sources. Have a matrix of possibilities showing worst, best and most realistic scenarios. This is critical because if your worst case scenario is unprofitable, then you have to do something before committing your second mortgage to a product launch. The realistic scenario allows you to plan your expenses wisely. The optimistic scenario gives you raw materials for pleasant daydreams.

Let's get back to the first two market sizing's. Once you have quantified the total market, you determine your addressable market by chipping away at the pie-in-the-sky estimates by bounding the total market with restrictive market forces.

Your first bounding is the **technology adoption lifecycle** – made famous by Moore and his Chasm crossing theory. The later in the adoption life cycle, the more mature the market, the smaller the remaining market and the higher the cost of penetration. We will talk much more about the product adoption lifecycle throughout Start-up CEO's Marketing Manual.

Market definition elements – bounding

- ## Bounding: the processes of reducing the total market by evaluating pressures that restrict sales

  - Technology adoption life cycle
  - Competition
  - Market disciplines of customers
  - Cost of sales into regions
  - Andrew Grove's six forces

  Total Market

  Addressable Market

The number and strength of competing offerings reduces the green field available to you. Going against Oracle in the database business is a much different struggle than inventing a new market with a new product. Oracle pretty much owns all the big accounts and the switching costs for customers all but kills opportunities for other database vendors (remember Ingress). In later life cycle markets, this is one of your most serious bounding vectors.

The market disciplines of B2B customers will also constrain you. We'll discuss market disciplines later, but know for now that your products likely amplify one or more of three market disciplines (product, operational and customer intimacy) which are the means by which your clients make money. If your product amplifies only one of the three, you generally cut your addressable market by 75%.

Finally, Andrew Grove – a former CEO of Intel and one of its earliest employees – defined six market forces which present a handy model for further bounding your addressable market. Since Intel has always been in highly competitive markets, let's dig deeper into Andy's six forces.

Market definition elements – Six Forces

- ## Andrew Grove – former Intel CEO
  - Competitors
  - Potential competitors
  - Complementors
  - Customers
  - Suppliers
  - Different ways of doing what you do

These market forces are conceptually simple. Measuring them is not:

Competition in all forms: Other products, non-products, governments and of course the competitive threat of customers being content with what they already have.

Potential competitors: Intel may have once considered mobile phone chips as a *potential* competitor until they realized that cell phones were becoming portable computers. As it happens, the ARM chip become a competitor to Intel in the server space once people realized that a massive collection of those chips were cheap and handled mundane web farm tasks quite well.

Complementors: These add strength to a product – yours or a competitor's. Make sure to look at both angles, to see if your product is a complementor to somebody else.

Customers: People and organizations are the ultimate force. They decide what the market wants because they are the market. The number of customers, their needs, wants, hopes, desires and aspirations, as well as the depth of their pockets, strongly define your markets.

Suppliers: These are a tricky force. Good suppliers, bad suppliers, too few suppliers, too many suppliers. If you depend on anyone to provide you the materials with which to make your product, this is a serious consideration, especially in industries where suppliers can be acquired by your competitors.

Different approaches: This market force is the least studied by start-ups, and oddly may be the most important force. There are always different ways to achieve a desired outcome, and odds are your customers are already using one or more of them. The status quo can be a barrier to entry.

Intuit faced an interesting problem when they originally launched Quicken. Few people wanted to database their checkbook entries. Quicken created extra work for most people and did not alleviate any real daily pain – well, except for people incapable of balancing their checkbook. Intuit discovered that what people really hated was writing checks. So Intuit started selling checks that customers could put in their printers, and once the bill payment data was entered a check would be typed. It was the different solution – to the manual writing of checks – that was a force. Intuit had to create an alternative to that force to make their core product successful.

Before moving on, I want to list some of the common traps start-ups encounter when performing a market definition. These are especially important to start-ups because not only are they sources of self-delusion, but they are the red flags for which investors watch. Say any of these during a funding pitch and you will likely get pitched out the door.

If we can get just 1% of the market ... A venture capitalist will instantly ask, "And how do you find, contact and sell to 1%?" When you define your market, knowing your addressable market and segment, having realistic expectations of how you market and sell to them, and what your average sales rate is will quantify your probability of success. All of these points must be defensible.

This is a hot market ... So is the market for dolls, but would you want to compete toe-to-toe with Barbie, a product that has been the worldwide favorite for 50 years and has sold over a billion units? Sometimes specialization and niche plays are your best option. Never assume you can or should try to sell into a market just because of *potential*. The pretty girl or handsome man at the end of the bar has potential ... they might also be drunk and psychotic.

We have no competition ... Everyone has competition. When Quicken was first introduced, nobody bought it. The competition Quicken faced was the status quo – the old-fashioned job of writing checks by hand. You have competitors and you better know *who* or *what* they are.

A billion units were sold last year ... Is this a sign of a growing or a saturated market? Why introduce a product into a market that has had its fill? Or worse, have any large competitors bought companies that might have a competing product (a possible sign of consolidation)? Markets change and you have to constantly be looking into the future.

We're relying on word of mouth ... So is everyone else. Do you know how buzz marketing works? Can you identify all the top influencers? How will you seed conversations? Why should influencers care? How many social media workers does this require? Wanting to sell to a million people is great; but do you know how to do that, and how much it will cost, and have you tested your campaigns? You better.

Your Action List

1. List what you don't know that you need to.
2. Review your business plan for common mistakes.
3. Put yourself in the VC seat and ask if you would invest in you given your current pitch.
4. Color code the master marketing matrix and see what on the left side needs attending to.
5. Reduce what you think your market is by bounding.

Chapter 2 – Segmentation

An old Chinese guy[3] once said "A journey of a thousand miles began with a single step."

The best way to dominate a market is to dominate one small piece of the market at a time. It is like devolving a complex project into a number of small steps or an elaborate PERT schedule. You can solve a smaller problem (e.g. dominating one part of a market) and in doing so solve the bigger one (dominating the entire market). Smaller market chunks are more manageable and have a smaller set of unified needs. Once you dominate one segment and can easily defend it, you can safely/profitably move to the next.

This is the chief goal of market segmentation, which is the process of dividing the *addressable* market into manageable segments.[4] Of everything you will learn in Start-up CEO's Marketing Manual, segmentation is arguably the most critical. Segment well, and you will grow smoothly and profitably. Segment badly, or not at all, and you'll be running against the wind until you die.

And death is overrated.

---

[3] His name was Lao Tzu. He was a revered 7th century philosopher, so naturally I had to poke fun at him.

[4] The smarter readers will realize that after segmenting, a number of segments will not be in their *realistic* market.

Let's itemize all the reasons you want to segment your market.

Segmentation – why do it

- Your addressable market is too big to sell
- Each segment has different specific needs
- Segmenting and prioritizing allows
  - Establishing a beachhead
  - Create a strong defensive niche
  - Develop sustaining revenues
- Dominate one segment then grow into adjacent segments

Sell small: Odds are your total market is huge – possibly every human with an Internet connection. You cannot sell to everyone – period. This is especially true if yours is a new product, a new market or a new technology. Segmenting allows you to sell to one piece of market, then another, then another.

Serially specialize: Each segment has a unique combination of needs. Addressing all the needs in a single segment allows you to create a *whole product* for that segment. This makes you unbeatable within that segment and thus guarantees a measure of safety and a revenue stream. Since many features necessary to dominate one segment are part of the whole product definition for other segments, you use your dominance in one segment to grow into neighboring segments by augmenting your product step-wise.

Prioritization: Segmenting allows you to visualize how to establish a beachhead in one segment where the competition is light, then grow into other segments. Setting segment-by-segment priorities provides safe, sane, planned growth. Soon enough you can crowd out competitors in all meaningful segments.

This system of establishing a beachhead in one segment, then expanding into neighboring segments causes what the folks at the Chasm Group have called the "bowling alley" phase of growth, where one pin is not knocked down by the bowling ball (you) but the neighboring pin (the preceding market segment).

This is the most important element of technology marketing you will ever learn: good segmenting leads to smart growth that blocks competition and accelerates your growth in a geometric way. Segment early, segment well, review often or die young.

Key to good segmentation is selecting a good **segmentation model**. Segmentation models are schemes for dividing the market based on naturally occurring clusters of buyers. Segmenting models are based on two stark realities.

Micro whole products: A segment has a unique whole product definition for buyers in that segment. These may overlap with other segments, which is where you find your next opportunities.

Automatic buzz: Buyers in a segment are self-referencing – they talk to one another and reinforce preferences. This was true long before social media. People with similar needs commune online and offline. Segmenting to put talkers into the same groups helps promote without obvious promotion.

A segmentation model has to conform to the specific needs of its market, and these are defined using relevant *vectors*. A segmentation vector is any measurable aspects of the needs and priorities of the buyers in the addressable market. For example, VA Software sought to commercialize SourceForge, a popular software development management portal. I led their team in examining what natural clusters of software developers or development organizations existed in the market. One natural segmentation vector was the programming language and platform combination (C++, Java, Windows, etc.). Interacting in a software development collaboration suite is facilitated in part by uniting it with the desktop environment of developers (their IDEs). Thus, programming languages and target platforms were natural software development collaboration market segmentation vectors.

Here is where segmentation gets complicated. You may have multiple vectors for modeling segments. You may end up with a multidimensional segmentation model that creates many, many, many possible segments. At the opposite end of the spectrum, you might have very horizontal products, have very few vectors and a small number of very simple segments. The point is that you must pick the vectors that actually matter in your market and not just some convenient default like industry verticals.

That being said, it is useful to examine some of the very common segmentation vectors. Keep in mind that these are just some *common* ones. Your segmentation model may use many of these or none of these. Your model will likely have vectors that are either uncommon or completely unique to your market.

Segmentation – common models

- Some common (but possibly inappropriate) segmentation models include:
  - Geography
  - Industry verticals
  - Platform/architecture
  - Theme or club (e.g., Open Source)
  - Profession or function
  - Business size
- Drop all prejudices about how to model

Geography: Often, either a product is not usable in some geographies, or the area is not ready for it. But often dividing a market by regions helps to prioritize regions in which to sell, or to map where your competitors are strong/weak.

Industry verticals: These are the various industries in common classification guides – industries like financial services, energy and manufacturing.

Business size: This is an often overlooked yet very important vector. If your product is designed to help large enterprises eke out fraction of a penny per unit profit margin, small businesses are not a market for you. Likewise, if your SaaS solution is geared toward easy payroll management, then big enterprises are not a segment for you either.

Two things to note: First, the more horizontal your product – the more it applies to everyone – the less these *common* vectors matter. An Intel-based server applies perfectly well to a small business and an enterprise or to a hair products manufacturer or an oil exploration company.

Segmentation – rules for validation

For each possible segment produced by a segmentation model, ask:

1) Is it "relevant" based on what you know about the broad market?
2) Are there definable, consistent attributes (locations, company size, etc.) ?
3) Is each segment self-referencing?
4) Are the needs and expected outcomes of buyers highly similar within each segment?
5) Are there "big fish in small pond" opportunities?

Second, drop your prejudices about segmentation. Forget any adherence to one model or another. As you explore what really makes up your market and how your competitors are approaching segmentation, the real vectors that make a difference in dividing your markets will become apparent. Let's see how to identify the right ones. There are five basic tests for deciding if a segmentation vector or model is right for your market.

Relevancy: The simplest test is simply, "Is it relevant?" When VA Software was launching SourceForge Enterprise edition, they originally wanted to divide the market by industry verticals. I asked, "Why are industry verticals relevant to your buyers or your competition?" Unable to answer, they dropped verticals as a segmentation vector.

Consistent buyer attributes: Buyers within resulting segments must have some similarities. The reason is that your whole product definition and your value propositions must be meaningful to the buyers, and this changes within each segment. If not, you cannot map similarities within each segment and you cannot build a whole product for the segments and thus can never find a sufficient number of buyers or defend against competitors.

Self-referencing: A segment must be composed of buyers who talk to one another. By sharing and having a common language and a common set of needs, they will talk about your products to one another and you can tailor your messages to segment members in order to start these conversations.

Expected outcomes: A segment should have buyers that generally want the same outcomes from using a product. Quicken (Intuit) divides their products between basic home accounting, people who invest, people who run small businesses and those who own/rent real property. People in each of these segments have different expected outcomes (balance my checkbook, maximize my returns, organize my business, make renting a house profitable).

Big fish, small pond: When a segmentation model exposes segments where you can be a big fish in a small pond – where you can become the dominate player quickly – then you have a model on which you can anchor your company. This big fish reality is hugely important to start-ups, but it is key to every new product. Establishing an unshakable, dominant claim in one or more segments means you will have the time and income to grow into other segments.

When I helped VA Software launch an enterprise edition of their legendary SourceForge software development portal, their segmentation model was based on the five rules and whittled down an original list of three dozen brainstormed vectors. The result was a 2D matrix based on:

> Software technology preferences (Windows, Java, C++, Pascal, COBOL, etc.)

Departmental types (IT applications, IT systems, mechanical engineering, mission critical, embedded, etc.)

These two vectors were supreme and could be further reduced for micro segmentation. Yes, you heard that right. Each segment can be divided into smaller segments. You might not need to do this, but if your market and product are complex, it may well be inevitable.

Segmentation – a case study

		Departmental			
		IT, MIS, IS	R&D and Engineering	Partnership management	Ad-hoc groups
	UNIX	Database-driven back-off applications	Middleware, internals, communications	Cross-product integration	Anything to the left
	Windows	End user applications, some server-side database work	Drivers, 3rd party products, hardware	Cross-product integration, UI collaboration, data interchange	Anything to the left
Technology Preferences	OS-400	Database-driven back-off applications	Drivers, 3rd party products, hardware	Cross-product integration	Anything to the left
	VMS	Database-driven back-off applications	Drivers, 3rd party products, hardware	Cross-product integration	Anything to the left
	Etc.				

This is a small portion of the segmentation study created for VA Software. Notice that a natural 2D matrix was developed for this product where the preference for platform and languages intersected with the type of software the customer developed. You can see how development managers overseeing Java development for enterprise applications reference one another, as do people creating desktop apps for Macs. Members of either group rarely converse with people in the other group. Later on we mapped the size of each segment, the competitive landscape and the product's strengths and weaknesses therein.

Without this basic understanding of your markets, you will spend vast sums of money chasing poor opportunities in segments that have few customers or no demand, or where the competition is too stiff. It is more important to carefully segment your market than to undertake any other strategic activity. More importantly, think about the people in each cell of your segmentation map and how they communicate to one another, within their company, within their industry and between industries. This commonality of daily discussion is what drives conversations, solution sharing and buzz, and buzz drives rapid growth.

Many start-ups fall into traps based on poor segmentation. The first trap is that nobody can sell to every segment at once. Not even IBM or Proctor and Gamble. They segment too and they do it well and are smart enough not to spread themselves thin.

The second trap is that start-ups do not have enough capital to sell to everyone, even with the help of the Internet. Even if they could "sell" to everyone, start-ups are not big enough to handle all those orders even if you could sell to everyone. How big is your tech support staff?

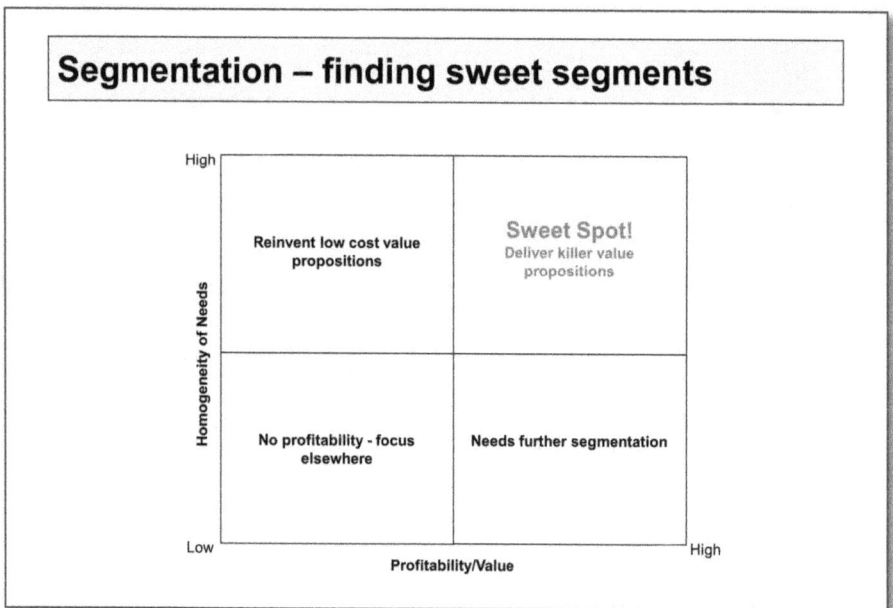

Segmentation – finding sweet segments

Reinvent low cost value propositions	**Sweet Spot!** Deliver killer value propositions	
No profitability - focus elsewhere	**Needs further segmentation**	

Homogeneity of Needs (High / Low)

Profitability/Value (Low / High)

However, start-ups can win enough business in one segment to dominate and defend it, and use those segment revenues to grow into the next segment. That is the key to survival – finding a beachhead, taking it, defending your high ground and marching on from there. The way you prioritize your first and early segments is to start with segments where your product offers the best whole product – where it matches more of the needs of buyers in that segment than any competing solution. This will gain you early revenue and rapidly create a defensible position.

That having been said, you need to weigh the profitability of a segment with whole product matching. If your best whole product match is in a segment with few buyers, unmotivated buyers or very strong competitors, then you may need to engineer your product for another segment where you can grow successfully. No use fishing in a dry lake.

Take those two concepts – whole product fit and profitability potential – and you will see an interesting reality in most markets (note, I said *most* — your reality may vary). Where there is a high homogeneity of needs — where everyone in the segment has the same expected outcomes — and the segment has good profitability potential is where you find a great segment in which to launch. If the segment has profit potential but the buyers do not have a distinct set of needs, that segment can be divided into subsegments where a niche sweet spot can be found. Do not fear subsegmenting – you will face it sooner rather than later.

Segmentation – segment scorecard

	Current Segment			Segment #1			Segment #2		
	Products	Services	Total	Products	Services	Total	Products	Services	Total
Revenues									
Base revs	1,230,000	220,000	1,450,000	990,000	70,000	1,060,000	80,700	145,000	225,700
Upsale potential									
New customers	123,000	22,000	145,000	99,000	7,000	106,000	8,070	14,500	22,570
Existing customers	61,500	11,000	72,500	49,500	3,500	53,000	4,035	7,250	11,285
Cross-sale potential									
New customers	86,100	15,400	101,500	89,300	4,900	74,200	5,649	10,160	15,799
Existing customers	0	0	-	0	0	-	0	0	-
Lost revs	0	0	0	0	0	0	0	0	0
	1,500,600	268,400	1,769,000	1,207,800	85,400	1,293,200	98,454	176,900	275,354
Fixed expenses									
Development	61,500		61,500	59,700		59,700	77,500		77,500
Variable expenses									
Marketing	150,060		150,060	97,000		97,000	9,845		9,845
Account management	15,006	2,684	17,690	12,078	854	12,932	986	1,769	2,754
Services		134,200	134,200		42,700	42,700		88,450	88,450
	226,566	136,884	363,450	168,778	43,554	212,332	88,330	90,219	178,549
Profitability			1,274,034			1,039,022			10,124
ROI			562%			618%			11%

When I lecture companies on segmentation, it is about now that someone asks "How do you know the profitability of any segment?"

One way is to devise and apply a scorecard to each segment, whereby you estimate each potential segment's top and bottom lines (revenues and costs) as well as growth potential. This scorecard shows the basics. Only include segments for which you have or can quickly create a whole product (it doesn't matter how potentially profitable a segment is if you don't provide the product buyers therein require).

Honesty is the trick to making segment scorecards. You cannot afford to do what many entrepreneurs have done – subconsciously misestimate revenues or costs in favor of the segment you happen to like. We all wear blinders and beer goggles. We all have favorites, be they market segments or children. The best way to avoid screwing-up your segmentation scorecards is to have someone outside of your company take your segment list and fill in the numbers for you. There is no phase of market strategy development more important than segmentation and objectivity is essential.

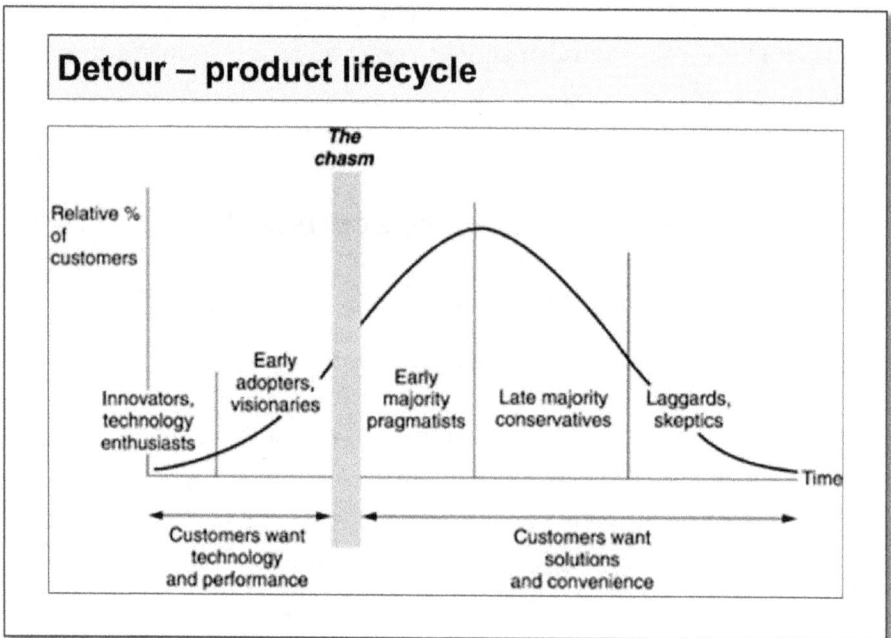

Detour – product lifecycle

Relative % of customers

The chasm

Innovators, technology enthusiasts

Early adopters, visionaries

Early majority pragmatists

Late majority conservatives

Laggards, skeptics

Time

Customers want technology and performance

Customers want solutions and convenience

No discussion of segmentation should avoid mentioning Crossing the Chasm.

If bits and pieces of my segmentation discussion sound familiar, you are right. The concepts of segmenting and creating a whole product solution to establish a beachhead in a key segment are fundamentals in Chasm Crossing theory, as popularized by Geoffrey Moore. The beachhead lies on the other side of a gulf that separates new technology ideas from buyers who, with the exception of brave early adopters, are not ready to buy. Finding your beachhead segment on the other side of the chasm is critical to success. At the risk of making too fine of a point, buy and read Moore's book. Over the years four or five books will be deeply important to you succeeding in the technology business. Moore's book is the second on that very short list (you are currently reading the first).

Another truth Moore detailed was that the market is segmented into different types of buyers who purchase products at different times during the lifespan of a product. This segmentation vector – market lifecycle – must always be included in your planning regardless of what other segmentation vectors you use. The motivations of buyers in the enthusiast, early adopter, early and late majority and laggard phases are important to how you find and sell to them. Know where in its lifecycle your market is before committing manpower and money, otherwise you will pick segments poorly and fade faster than Friday night sitcoms.

Your Action List

1. List your essential segmentation vectors and make sure they are valid.
2. Map your market maturity phase and know how that affects buyer motivations.
3. Prove that your segments are self-referencing.
4. Prove that you are targeting profitable segments and not fighting through commodity segments.

Chapter 3 – Genotypes

I co-opted the word *genotype*, plagiarizing the biological science lexicon. I use the term to describe people to whom you will communicate while marketing your products. The word in biology is defined as "the genetic makeup of an organism or group of organisms with reference to a single trait, set of traits, or an entire complex of traits."

Genotypes

- Defined: Unique buying decision influencers within a segment of a specific market
- Multiple people often influence a decision to buy
- Each has different motivations and power
- You must communicate to all of them
- In B2B they can often be grouped by job titles

In marketing a genotype[5] is a class of humans who *influence* the decision to buy a product and who have similar traits. When selling anything more complex than tap water there are two or more people who influence the decision. This applies to consumer goods and business software. Has your child ever begged for a particular brand of breakfast cereal they saw advertised on TV? When choosing a cereal there are two buyer genotypes involved: your kid and you.

But your kid's motivations and yours were completely different. They want the colorful dancing cartoon characters and the 500% USRDA sugar content. You want to feed them something healthy, but you also want them to shut up about the cereal. Notice that on Saturday morning cartoons the cereal company sells fun. But their packaging — what you encounter on the grocery store shelf — mentions "whole grain" on the front of the box. The cereal company understood both buyer genotypes (children and parents) and communicated to them about different product features (fun and whole grains) through the optimal media for each (TV and packaging). This is genotype definition, motivation analysis and outbound communications in a nutshell.

Once you know your market and your target segments, you have to identify *everyone* who influences the buy decision (and if you don't think your kids *influence* which breakfast cereals you buy, then you are not paying attention). You must map their different motivations and how they prefer to receive information. You will need to communicate to each of them and sell to each of them.

In B2B sales, you can often classify genotypes by job titles. This works well enough that it at least is a good starting point if not an end-all. Let's look at traditional IT shops for an example.

In most IT organizations there are three basic levels in the departmental hierarchy: executives who are in charge of strategy, mid-level managers who are in charge of executing executive strategy and keeping the systems up, and techies who have to live with the technology that has been implemented. Depending on the phase of the market's lifecycle and the cost of the product, any or all of these people may be in on a purchase decision. You need to know who has a voice and what

---

[5] The term *personae* is often used for this concept.

kind of influence they exert. You have to know their individual motivations, and you have to market to each of them individually.

The power that a genotype has is important. Propose a system that the techies despise, and the push back will be so great that CIO will not buy the solution for fear of functional mutiny. So for each genotype, take the time to know if they can mandate a solution regardless of the other genotypes, or if other genotypes can functionally veto a decision. Mandating or vetoing can be done at any level — techies quite often mandate while executives rubber stamp the decision. I'm sure at some time or another both you and your spouse have mandated and vetoed a purchase decision — you mandated which car to buy and she vetoed the bachelor party in Vegas.

Genotypes – common B2B IT genotypes

- In IT, there are three common genotypes
  - CxO – strategic decision makers
  - Directors/managers responsible for implementing strategy
  - Techies who have to live with the solution
- Power
  - Some genotypes can mandate technologies
  - Some genotypes can veto technologies
  - They can be on the top or the bottom
- Leadership
  - Sometimes people on the bottom lead adoption

Be acutely aware that power always comes from the ranks. Executives only have as much power as plebiscites let them get away with. Often the lowest ranks implement technologies without the direction or even consent of their bosses. Linux remains the poster child for the lowest tech caste acquiring technologies that later dominated the market.

In order to effectively market/communicate to each buyer genotype, you must first map the motivations of each and you must examine both their functional and emotive motivations and demotivations. The human brain is composed of functional (rational) and emotional forces, and no human is devoid of either.

Functional motivations are those that relate to mechanical value being delivered. Saving money, maintaining uptime. These are functional outcomes.

Emotive motivations are personal in nature and reflect what the genotype wants for themselves and not necessarily for their company or family. Less stress, greater self-esteem, more sex appeal. These are emotive.

Genotypes – motivation mapping

- All genotypes have functional and emotional motivations and demotivations
- Itemize all the common and powerful motivations
- Motivations common to all genotypes become headlines
- Motivations specific to one genotype appear in specialized collateral or field sales messages
- Often their "expected outcomes" are both motivators and product features

Left Brain	Right Brain
Linear	Creative
Yin	Yang
Dark	Light
Tangible	Abstract
Logical	Intuitive
Incremental	Transformational
Rigid	Random
Process Theory	Chaos Theory
Mathematics	Art
Function	Form
Control	Influence
Vanilla	Chunky Monkey
Microsoft	Apple

iPod advertising is a great example of tapping into emotive motivations. When introduced, Apple could have appealed to the audiophile or music enthusiast by hyping the iPod's broad and flat frequency response and other spec sheet boredom inducing elements, which would have shown iPods to be little better than existing and cheaper music players. Apple instead advertised happy, dancing silhouettes that said, "Let your joy out through music." Apple tapped into the emotional side of promotions because studies have shown emotions to be more powerful than logic. This even applies to heartless CIOs and spec-happy CTOs.

After you itemize the motivations and demotivations for all active genotypes in your target segments, look for common threads between them. Common motivations across all important genotypes are your headlines and top value propositions (in other words, the one pitch to hook them all). Don't be worried if the primary common motivator for your B2B IT infrastructure product is an emotional motivator. If it is common and strong, put it in big, bold type on the top of your landing page.

Playing to both halves of the brain is important, though not as important as once perceived. Studies have shown that promotions based on emotion do better than campaigns based on logic alone or a combination of logical and emotional elements. If your product is technical, you will have to appeal to rational motivations eventually – after all, techies do check specs. But opening invitations to investigate are best driven by the gut.

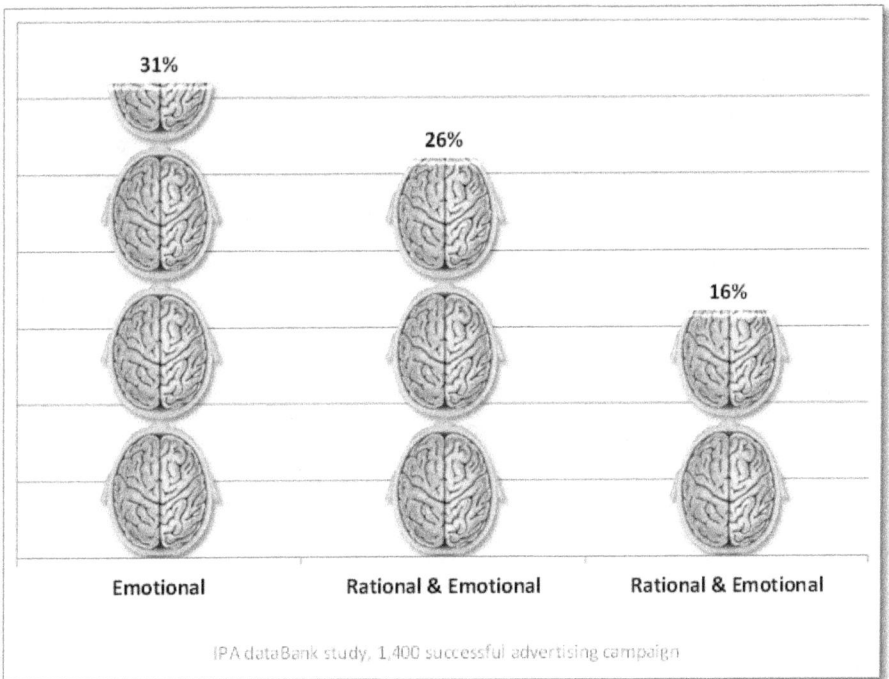

31%   26%   16%

Emotional   Rational & Emotional   Rational & Emotional

IPA dataBank study, 1,400 successful advertising campaign

Here is a good case study on how emotive motivators make a difference. Telamon sold software that caused people's pagers (remember those?) to go off in the middle of the night, during dinner and all those times when support staff really would like them not to – you know, that stuff we call life. Telamon's products plugged into network monitoring stacks like HP Openview, help desk systems, and other enterprise IT management tools.

While devising Telamon's go-to-market strategy, I listed the genotypes of everyone that influenced the decision to buy IT management and help desk solutions and reviewed their motivations. This included network engineers, server jockeys and help desk operators to name a few. The common thread between all these genotypes was stress. They had high-stress jobs. Reducing their stress was an emotionally based expected outcome. They wanted to be happier.

We created two magazine advertisements (remember those?). One graphically showed what the product did and the other showed a typical looking corporate IT slave jumping for joy. Telamon ran the ads in the same magazines and added up measurements (bingo cards, reader response surveys, etc.) The "happy jumping man" advertisement out-scored the technical/rational ad on recall and interest by about 26%. On-call people in IT were more motivated by making work life less painful than they were by how the pain was alleviated.

More to the point, the "peace of mind" promotions appealed to the common emotional motivator of all the important genotypes. Focusing the international campaign on selling "peace of mind" drove revenues from an average of 5% annual growth to 23% annually in the first year (well, actually the first nine months). Yes, there were other marketing activities, but they too were tied to the global Telamon "peace of mind" brand and promise. Never underestimate the power of emotions for they have started wars, caused children and marriage (often in that order) and made you buy an iPod before you knew what one was.

Incidentally, the Telamon "bang head here" mouse pads were very popular and are allegedly still on people's desk 20 years later.

Genotypes – motivation mapping

Genotype	Motivators	Demotivators
CIO	•Meeting *corporate-wide* goals and market demand initiatives (business alignment) by proactively envisioning business opportunities •Achieving the goals faster, to stay ahead of the competition •Effectively managing ad hoc developers – contractors and outsourcers – as well as their internal teams to reduce costs •Integrate existing and new systems •Clearing the application backlog	•Vendor lock-in •Distraction from business issues and how technology can help achieve them – *firefighting decreases my time for strategic planning* •Lack of quality – *I cannot invest in tools that don't help meet corporate objectives*
CTO	•Architecting corporate-wide infrastructures that reduce mistakes and costs •Reducing the number of technologies and unifying systems •Open standards-based technologies	•Non-standard products – *My job is to standardize everything, including tools and processes. Don't break that.* •Non-extensible, non-integratable products •Anything not based on open standards, if not actually open source •Scalability – *Apps tend to grow out of control and I am in charge of making sure things work well and don't lock us in or out* •We don't have time to learn yet another technology
Application manager	•Meeting growing application demands •Getting more code written without more budget •Higher developer productivity •Less maintenance time, expense and distraction •Shortening development time and reducing development steps •Team management with outsourcing – collaboration is becoming a huge issue •Fast design/feature acceptance by customers/users •Easily adapt to changing requirements without heavy reengineering •Integration, integration, integration •Measuring developer productivity and success (metrics)	•Non-portable programming talent – need to keep team members working with a small set of technologies •Insecure methodologies – *I'm under a lot of governance pressures* •Quality can't suffer •Tools have to encourage documentation – *Prototyping and RAD tools tend to leave this out. I need to preserve understanding of "why" as much as "how"* •Can't be trapped by scalability, bugs, or the inability to tweak the application to exacting needs
Application developer	•Better understanding of user requirements before coding •Focus on the business issues and not the technology details •More fluid development process •Can prototype and develop simultaneously	•*Don't waste my time; I'm under pressure to write code!* •*I like playing with the code. Don't block me from the details.* •Management has unrealistic expectations of what prototyping/RAD/etc deliver. I don't want to be penalized because they read a sharp sales brochure with lofty promises.

Let's get back to mapping all those genotypes to whom you will promote your products. The table shows an example of a genotype motivation map that I did for a software development tool company.

Notice that I identified four genotypes and for each listed both motivators and demotivators. This level of mapping is basic to discovering where similarities in motivations bridge genotypes and lead you to create top-line value propositions and messages. The process for generating a motivation map that is accurate is more complex than can be discussed here, but know that many navel-gazing start-ups fail to accurately capture motivations, and instead project the founder's beliefs about buyers onto genotypes. If in doubt, have someone survey the market and determine what their motivations actually are.

Demotivators are also important to your marketing efforts. If a genotype is demotivated to buy your solution, you must address their fears, reservations or complaints. This may be as simple as providing proof points or as painful as reengineering part of your product. But all serious demotivators must be addressed or they create insurmountable roadblocks. If the same demotivations are reflected in your competitors' products, there is no shame in subtlety point this out to buyers.

An aside to demotivations, and to all things negative, it is important

Genotypes – motivation mapping

IT	CIO	• Meeting *corporate-wide* goals and market demand initiatives (business alignment) by proactively envisioning business opportunities Diff-1.2: Most unmet corporate goals are getting people within the organization to work together more effectively. Xxx's ability to rapidly go from idea, to prototype, to deployment makes both ad hoc and structured work-flow apps easy to write quickly. • Achieving business goals faster, to stay ahead of the competition Diff-1: Visualizing business interactions in an intuitive application development environment to reach these goals sooner. Not just the conceptual prototyping, but the deployment and *inevitable* maintenance when business objectives change. • Effectively managing ad hoc developers – contractors and outsourcers – as well as their internal teams to reduce costs • Integrate existing and new systems • Clearing the work backlog Diff-1.2.6: Xxx's intuitive and schema-less design system allows both hyper-RAD development, but also the option of end-user self-development.	• Vendor lock-in Diff-5: Xxx's Open Source foundation and community portal reduces vendor lock-in risk. • Distraction from business issues and how technology can help achieve them – firefighting decreases my time for strategic planning. Diff-6: The integration of Xxx's frameworks eliminates incompatibility panics. The Xxx delivers end-to-end application development without firefighting over non-compatible solution sets. • Lack of quality – I cannot invest in tools that don't help meet corporate objectives.

during market message creation that language that which echoes demotivators be corrected or removed. Never include negatives in marketing messages unless they are used creatively to demonstrate the positive aspects of your products. Too many marketers lean on amplifying buyer pain points instead of articulating the delivered value. We pay for value, not to be reminded of what we loathe.

Once all genotype motivations have been documented, you look for commonalities between them. In this example we color-coded motivators and matched each motivator to the product's differentiators. Intersections between what the market is **motivated** to achieve (their expected outcomes) and how a product is **different** from competing solutions is where rapid market acquisition occurs.

As an aside, the painful lesson many start-ups learn is that if you cannot match market motivators to your product differentiations then you must create new differentiation. Hyping what you can do that your competitors can also do is slow-motion bankruptcy. Likewise, hyping things you cannot do is brand destruction.

Genotypes – motivation mapping

Dept.	Genotype	Differentiators							
		1	2	3	4	5	6	7	8
IT	CIO	✓	✓	✓	✓	✓	✓	✓	✓
IT	CTO	✓	✓	✓	✓	✓	✓		✓
IT	Application manager	✓	✓	✓	✓		✓	✓	✓
IT	Application developer	✓	✓	✓	✓		✓		✓
INDY	Business management								
INDY	Development management	✓	✓				✓		✓
INDY	Developer								
Summary		5	5	4	4	2	5	2	5

Hyping non-motivators (those things that in no way motivate target genotypes) is delusional. Many start-ups lie to themselves. They dream up nonexistent motivations to match their product's differentiators.

This is mainly a founder defect, caused when an entrepreneur sees a beautiful combination of technologies and features that they can turn into a product, but for which they never measured demand or studied non-product competition. They are actually shocked to learn that elegant design and bleed-edge technology does not necessarily produce a meaningful outcome for buyers. Understand that the coolest idea will flop if it does not help people achieve what it is *__they__* want to achieve – their motivations – not your vision.

There is one last step in mapping genotype motivations. Do a count of which genotypes have motivations that matched product differentiation. Where many genotypes share a motivation is where you design products. Where many genotypes share motivations and you provide their expected outcomes, you have short sales cycles. In this example it is clear that motivations five and seven are not worth promoting to customers because few of the genotypes cared. However, headlining differentiators 1, 2, 6 and 8 made sense because all the genotypes were motivated by features that the product offered.

Your Action List

1. For each target segment, map everybody who influences the buy decision.
2. Map genotypes' emotional and rational motivations.
3. Find the common motivations and match them to your product differentiation.
4. Make these intersections your headline value propositions.

Chapter 4 – Whole Product Definition

A whole product is one that meets *all* the needs, wants and desires of the buyer.

Outside of clean water and fresh air, this is impossible – even air and water quality are questionable. When you take all the different

---

Whole Product – why and how

- Makes product easy to *buy*
  - A lack of objections to a product greases purchase decisions
- Block competition
  - Meeting customer goals is the best way to defeat competition
- Build brand preference
  - Happy customers promote your products
  - Biasing pre-sales decisions through buzz creates prejudicial customers

markets, different segments and different genotypes together, there are too many combinations of features, services, outcomes and prices to make *everyone* happy, so don't try. It is better to make 100 buyers very happy than 1,000 buyers largely dissatisfied. Again, this is why segmentation is so critical: the whole product needs of a single segment are — for practical purposes — obtainable.

The goal then is to carefully pick your target segment, create the best possible product — a whole product — for it. Dominate that segment then expand into the next most similar segment by augmenting your product or developing a new one.

Whole Product

- **Defined: Products that meet all the needs of the buyers in a segment or market**
  - This includes all
    - Features
    - Expected outcomes
    - Services
    - Price
    - Delivery
    - Etc., etc., etc.
- **The whole product definition is likely different for every segment and genotype**
- **Nobody ever creates a whole product, but they try getting closer all the time**

You need to worry about your whole product definition because it makes buying your product easier. Don't try to make your products easy to sell — make them easy to buy via lowering all points of friction and resistance. A 99¢ song downloaded directly into your smart phone and charged to your cellular bill is a product that is easy to buy. The fewer objections any genotype has to a product, the more rapidly it is adopted. A lot of sales people beg marketing departments to make their products easier to sell. Marketing's job is to make it easier to buy and to turn sales people into order takers.

The other goal to creating whole products for targeted segments is to block competition. If you have the closest thing to a segment's whole product, then buyers will largely ignore your competitors. If you meet buyers' expectations about outcomes, services, price and support, your competitors will suffer from vending an incomplete offering.

The long-range benefits are astounding. If you have a whole product for a segment, you build in that segment great brand preference (if not brand religion). It is easier to spread that brand preference to other segments when the time comes. In fact, a segment full of happy customers will do that for you, often before you are ready for them to do so.

Whole Product – four ways to assemble one

- ## There are many ways of creating whole products
  - – Build: **Create required features**
  - – Buy or borrow: **Acquire technology to complete the whole product**
    - • Open Source speeds whole product assembly
  - – Partner: **Augment with other companies' products and services**
  - – Ignore: **Explain why the customers' concern is not critical**

Keep in mind that a whole product is the sum of all _**possible**_ elements that together deliver all the expected outcomes of the buying genotypes. This includes not only product features, but business relationship features as well. Would you buy enterprise software without a support contract? Reliable service, support and bug fixes are part of the product. Interestingly, you don't have to deliver all the whole product features nor do it all yourself. You do, however, have to present a reasonably complete set of features as a unified solution set to buyers. In this you have several alternatives:

You can **build** the pieces of the product. In fact the core of your product is most likely something you built. This is the slowest and most costly approach, but the approach in which you likely must begin, especially if your product is disruptive.

You can **buy** or even **borrow** some part of the whole product. When WebTrends reinvented their small business product they used Windows versions of the Apache web server, MySQL database and a lot of other Open Source software to create a whole product that installed on your PC. Oracle became the IBM of the new millennia via buying most of their infrastructure components by acquiring whole companies.

Partnering has long been a favorite in the high-tech business. Half of Silicon Valley was built on strategic partnerships. Many people have made good money simply inventing parts of someone else's whole product. Take the Telamon example earlier — the software that sent pager notifications from other software. Telamon completed the whole product offering for HP Openview, IBM Tivoli, BMC Patrol and CA Unicenter. Alone Telamon's product had almost no market. In fact, after reading a magazine review of HP's Windows-based version of Open View, which complained of no pager notification function, and all I had to do to make HP's product manager partner with Telamon was to send him a copy of the article and use the phrase "incomplete whole product."

Lastly, you can **ignore** a part of the whole product definition. If some feature delivers few customers or is impossibly expensive to deliver, then you can ignore it. When looking at your whole product definition, decide for each element which is the wisest move – build, buy, partner or ignore. Odds are you will find faster and cheaper ways of getting your product to market or into a market dominating stature.

As already noted, a true whole product is impossible. This begs the question, "What kind of product can be created?" There are several layers of "whole" products, and it is worth noting the classification so you know what kind of product you currently offer and what are its prospects.

Generic products meet the minimal acceptable criteria for buying. Generics are just that – utterly lacking in differentiation between competitors. Ever read aspirin bottles? They are, for all practical purposes, 100% identical. Note though that generic products may also be new ones for which there are no competitors. The *only* solution is by definition the generic solution though unlike multi-competitor generic markets, it does not compete on price.

Expected products are those that meet the expected (as opposed to minimally acceptable) outcomes. Take steaks. A slab of stringy beef from a scrawny Texas longhorn is the generic product. It is red cow flesh that tastes kinda like steak. But a sirloin from a Hereford satisfies the taste buds and the nose, is more tender and has higher fat content. The Hereford steak is the expected product.

Now take a top-grade Angus steak (can you tell my family owned an Angus ranch?). The flavor is rich. The marbling is beautiful. It sizzles on the plate louder. It smells like you walked into heaven's kitchen. That is the **augmented** product. It lights up every sense in the body – sight, smell, touch, taste – and amplifies the sensations to the point of creating delirium. It goes beyond the customer's basic expectation.

Whole Product – the layers

- Generic
  - The minimal acceptable product and one that competes on price
- Expected
  - Product that meets all basic customer expectations within a segment
- Augmented
  - Product that fulfills most of the desires of key influencers
- Potential
  - What the perfect product for all buyers would be … which is entirely impossible

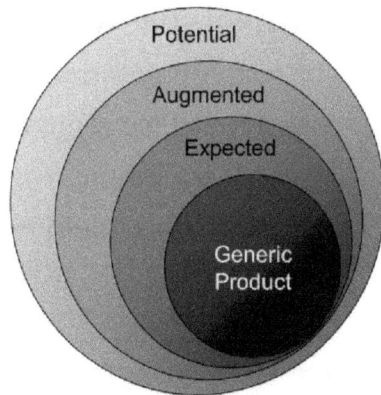

Potential

Augmented

Expected

Generic Product

Know in which of these groups your products and your competitor's products reside. Know what you need to add to your product to reach the next ring.

So how do you discover what the whole product is? Many entrepreneurs start developing products based on their observations of the market and how some task is not easily accomplished — in other words, they happened upon a desired outcome that had no available solution. Others entrepreneurs talked to cohorts and discovered frustrations or desired outcomes that could not be achieved. This was their start toward fulfilling a whole product definition.

The best initial method for identifying a whole product (typically once the generic product has been conceptualized) is through deep interviews. This non-trivial[6] technique is one where you probe buyer genotypes, driving the discussion to discover what expected outcomes they have for an activity, which can be a challenge because buyers do not always know what they want to achieve or have preconceived notions of how to do something which masks their actual expected outcome. You do not seek to understand what tools you or they envision using, but what they — the buyers — expect the outcomes of their labors to be.

Whole Product – discovering the definition

- Deep interviews
    - Good for determining the *expected outcomes*
    - Not good for statistically significant insights
    - Requires highly trained interviewers
    - Interviews should never be conducted by your employees (including you) who will bias what they hear

---

[6] Deep interview techniques require significant training to do correctly.

Expected outcomes are your targets. When you help buyers achieve a set of outcomes, you have created an *expected* product. The key is to look for the expected *outcomes*. Never talk about features because everyone, including the buyer, has preconceived notions about how to accomplish something. Talk about what the end *result* should be.

When you cleanly document discovered expected outcomes, your engineers and other creative people can devise the best way to achieve them. A customer may specify a knife to cut their steak. But if their expected outcome is to slice through a 2" thick Angus porterhouse with zero effort, an angle-serrated blade made from surgical steel might do better than a generic "steak knife."

Deep interviews are only the starting point to defining your whole product. They will tell you most of the expected outcomes your product could deliver. However, interviews tell you nothing about aggregate demand.

Whole Product – discovering the definition

- ## Surveying
  - Surveys provide broad, quantitative insights but do not provide important nuances
  - Poll each genotype and poll *non-customers*
  - Survey *all* genotypes that significantly influence buy decisions, track separately
  - Surveying is useful in deciding if competitor features are actually important

---

You will discover that genotypes have either endless or conflicting expected outcomes, and that you would never be able to fulfill them all. You need numbers in order to prioritize features. Specifically, you need to know what expected outcomes are most important to the most number of key buyer genotypes. It is better to deliver 10 features that are highly important to all genotypes than 90 features that are relatively unimportant or only important to a few people.

This is where **surveying** comes into play. Whereas deep interviews help to define an expected, augmented or even potential product, surveying identifies in what order to deliver the features that create expected outcomes. Interviews provide perspective and nuance. Surveys create product roadmaps.

When surveying, it is important to not survey your existing customers. Odds are they bought your product because it was at least a generic if not an expected product for them, meeting many of *their* specific expected outcomes. You want to find, interview and survey people who have not experienced your product and have no preconception about its ability to solve their problems. Ask them to rate the importance of all the expected outcomes to discover the most urgent items on your product roadmap. You'll often be surprised to discover that your competitors are chasing unimportant features. If they are, you know how to end their suffering.

Customer feedback tells you little about the broader market, one with non-customers and people who bought your competitor's products. After all, existing customers are people who have bought or tried your products and are telling you specifically what they experienced. It is a mistake to rely primarily on customer feedback. Such feedback is limited to your current product and how it does or does not serve part of the market and how this leads to creating minor enhancements for otherwise happy customers.

However, existing customers are good sources for two important pieces of information: what is great about your product and where it stinks. Places where your product shines, where people show inordinate delight – those are your strong differentiators and likely places where you are achieving the customer's expected outcomes. These are elements you want to promote today. Places where they complain loudly are the weaknesses that your competitors will harp on to create sales-engagement fear. These are elements you need to fix, or convince customers that they are unimportant.

It can be difficult to get customers to talk openly and honestly about your products to *you*. They will tell their peers. They will tell strangers. They will tell me when I conduct satisfaction surveys for you. Watch comments on social media sites or hire an external firm to measure your customer satisfaction. If you hear things through intermediaries that you are not hearing directly from your customers, you have a trust deficit situation with your own customers. That can be fatal.

Let's examine social networking and buzz as a tool for discovering your whole product.

Whole Product – discovering the definition

- ## Buzz monitoring
  - Buzz (word of mouth) networks are now very visible, fast and powerful
  - Peer-to-peer buzz is extremely honest
  - Good source for
    - Learning about positive or negative feedback
    - Getting feedback from non-customers (people who demo but don't buy)
    - Great for learning the same about your competitors
  - Buzz management is now essential for all companies

Peers talk — endlessly and to one another. They talk about your products, your competitor's products, related products, related services and the exact color of the sky in their neighborhood. Peers have always done this. Today however, their conversations are public – online, to a million "friends" and permanently archived. They can see it, you can see it and your competitors can see it.

This fact — that conversations are now public — is one of the great underutilized tools for whole product definition. Often while discussing work (not products) with peers, people say what it is they are trying to accomplish – what their expected outcomes are. They will also openly discuss what they hate about their current situation, which identifies new products, features and opportunities. They also use a common language that you should employ in your marketing collateral and your search engine optimization.

Buzz management is essential for staying competitive, and it is also an essential for better guiding your whole product research. Be part of these conversations, or at the very least, monitor them.

So let's recap how you go about developing a whole product definition. This is not the same as developing a whole product, but it does itemize what the market and your customers/competitors are striving for.

Whole Product – discovering summary

- **Deep interviewing**
  - Discovering what customers really want
- **Surveying**
  - Discovering how many customers want it
- **Buzz monitoring**
  - Discovering who is doing it well or not
- **Customer feedback**
  - Discovering what you are doing badly

Deep interviews and social media are the best tools for discovering the customer's expected outcomes that together are the whole product.

Surveying identifies how urgent each expected outcome is and helps you prioritize product roadmaps.

Buzz monitoring can discover what products/features are working or not, and what is missing from everyone's whole product definition.

Customer feedback is good for identifying what your product does well or badly, but given the human nature to complain more than praise, mainly it identifies what vendors don't deliver.

But whole products have one nasty side effect. They change.

Whole Product – per segment

	First Segment	Second Segment	Third Segment	Fourth Segment	Fifth Segment
Feature #1	✓	✓	✓	✓	✓
Feature #2		✓			
Feature #3				✓	✓

Fulfill all the requirements of the first segment before working on the second. Otherwise you leave your base vulnerable to attack from competitors.

It is better to have a secure base than rapid, careless growth

A whole product is different for every segment into which you can sell. Every feature — each of which should deliver one or more customer expected outcomes — may or may not be applicable to any given segment. Your whole product definition changes as the number of, and priority of, market segments changes.

That is why the beachhead strategy is vital. Once you have secured your beachhead and have a reasonably safe revenue stream, you can add features for your next segment that were not essential to your beachhead segment. Perform interviews and surveys of your next few segments to find their expected outcomes. If you discover high-priority features that address multiple segments, you may have a fast path to broad market dominance. If not, focus on those urgent features that are essential to the next segment on your list.

Would you like for your whole product definitions development to be more complicated? Too bad, it is.

The technology adoption life cycle influences whole product definitions. The essential features and outcomes necessary to satisfy innovators and early adopters are small and highly focused, solving specific niche issues. They are a foundation for early life cycle phases, but the larger whole product — the grand set of combined features that serves all segments — are not required early on. As markets mature and as your product becomes important to more and more buyers — as you move through the early and late majority phases — you will grow into other segments and add the features that those segments require for their whole product. The two — life cycle phases and segment-by-segment whole product definitions —are codependent.

Your Action List

1. Prioritize your segments.
2. Interview key genotypes in the target segment to discover their expected outcomes.
3. Survey many of the same genotypes to see which outcomes are urgent and unfulfilled.
4. Measure customer feedback to see when you are failing to meet expected outcomes.
5. Monitor buzz to find new opportunities.

Chapter 5 – Positioning

Positioning is a bipolar process. It has two distinct and related functions with entirely different purposes, they being:

Knowing **where your product is** against competitors using metrics/vectors important to customers.

Determining **where to take your product** in the future based on the same metrics.

Market definition elements – Positioning

- Positioning: identifying where in the market your product resides compared to competitor offerings
- Should include current and next-step positions
  - For the entire market
  - For your prioritized segments
- We'll cover positioning in more detail later today

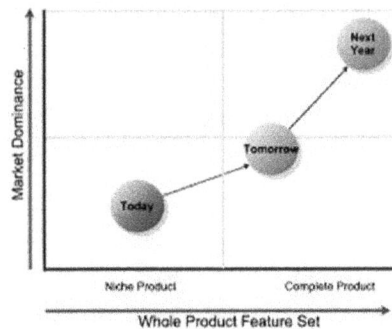

Positioning helps to clarify where *the market perceives* your products to be when compared to competitors, where it actually is and where you want people to think it is. These are three very odd and oddly important concepts.

First, your product lives on a grid (possibly an n-dimensional matrix, but let's stick to basics for now). As the Irish like to say, it is what it is – it does what it does and the same applies to your competitors. Knowing the *reality* of your and other products and how they compare on important customer-centric criteria tells you your current competitive situation. Knowing the reality often requires outside help because people too close to a product (that would be you and your staff) perceive it from their viewpoint, which is often not based in hard-nosed reality.

However, your product's real position may not be what the market thinks it is. Before I revised SuSE Linux's North American strategy, the market perceived SuSE to be a quirky foreign Linux distribution. The fact that SuSE Linux had excellent engineering and advanced administrative tools, and that from an operational standpoint it was superior to all other Linux distributions was lost on the market. Knowing your product's real position and if/how that differs from market perception is valuable because it shows if you have to battle a brand perception issue or if your brand is taking your product forward.

Aside from where your product is positioned today, you have two forward-looking positioning activities. The first is *making the market believe* what you want them to believe about your position (hopefully you are wise enough to know that the distance between your real position and what you tell the market to believe has to be short – stretch the truth too much and your brand will break and backlash like an overly taut rope). The other positioning activity is to plan your development agenda to change your product's real positioning in a way that minimizes competitive situations while maximizing customer acquisition and revenues. Going toe-to-toe with Oracle is unwise, though nibbling away at the periphery of one of their markets could eventually cause them to suffer. It is a long-range circle-and-strangle process, but one that works well.

You should reevaluate your positioning often and move your position through areas where competition is lightest. If your product inhabits a part of the market that has many strong competitors, you may opt to change your product to a less competitive quadrant. This allows you to build market share, momentum and revenues with the least friction and threat while constantly building a *whole product* that the broad market wants.

Positioning is almost exactly what it sounds like — locating or defining the position of your product on a map. The map is your market and like the old game of Battleship — your competitors are on the same map and trying to torpedo you.

In positioning remember that perception *is* reality as far as customers are concerned. Where on a market map your product is and where buyers and competitors think it is, are often two different things. How they perceive you drives their purchasing bias. Companies often position their product's brand perception in their next desired real position ahead of product updates (in other words, shape brand perception that the product already serves a segment or set of needs in advance of the product actually doing so). This is not a stunt for amateurs, but can be very effective in blunting competitor FUD.[7]

In the technology business there are many vendors who — from their websites and PR — look huge and very successful, and they are little more than two guys in a garage. There are also large and successful firms that look small and insignificant. Unmasking false perceptions is difficult but important not only in exposing your competitors, but also in not deluding yourself and your prospects. Accurate assessment of competitive positioning is essential both to avoid strategic product development mistakes and to communicate well to the market about you and your competitors.

Also understand that your position changes when either your products, your markets or your competitors change. One reason vendors like to redefine and reinvent markets is that it often knocks competitors completely off the positioning map, making them less relevant or even utterly irrelevant. If you are losing the game, change the rules.

There are five key points to product and corporate positioning:

---

[7] Fear, Uncertainty and Doubt, a common means for convincing buyers that a competing product is unworthy or risky.

Positioning – five points of knowledge

- Knowing what map to use
- Knowing where you are
- Knowing where your competition is
- Knowing where the market places you
- Knowing your next move

First you have to know what is your market map. If you are in San Francisco and you only have a map of Manhattan, then you have the wrong map and will be hopelessly lost. If your market is driven by factors X and Y and you are using a default map created by some industry analyst with A and B vectors, then you have no idea where you and your products are.

Next, you need to know where on the map you are. This is not trivial. Analyzing your position requires a great deal of honesty and discipline. Having the right map makes finding your position easier and more reliable. Dispelling internal bias about your product is mandatory and nearly impossible. Positioning analysis best left to outside experts.

On the same map you need to discover where competitors are, including non-product solutions. Companies often discover that competitors are not competitors when a market-defined positioning map shows them to be in different markets or segments. Even more often it will show non-product solutions to be significant competitors. A lot of technology companies died quickly because they did not map non-technical solutions as competitive threats. Remember, the status quo is always a competitive force.

Though not essential, at least in the early stages, it is important to know where on the map the market perceives you and your products. The market's perception is most important because if the perception is strong enough, the position the market perceives you to occupy will be the one that you do occupy, regardless of what your product actually does and what value it delivers.

Positioning – understanding a matrix

- ## Positioning is mapped on a matrix
- ## The axes are the primary motivation vectors of your customers
- ## Positioning matrixes can have more than two dimensions
- ## Positioning *is* different for each segment
  - ### But when your position is similar across segments, you have distinct advantages going forward

---

Finally, seeing your next destination on the map is essential to wisely planning how to get there. It's like using Google maps to create driving directions that provide the shortest path. Research and development is expensive. Spending R&D funds to enter small or highly competitive positions is an expense with little or no resulting revenue. Knowing where you are going is good, but it is even better to know where you should be going.

The most difficult part of positioning is getting the right map. Geographical maps are composed of vectors like north/south and east/west. Product positioning maps also have vectors. However, the vectors are different for every market if not for every segment in every market.

When choosing vectors by which to measure positions, pick vectors that are meaningful to your customers, not your product. Like everything else in marketing, the customer viewpoint is all that matters. The positioning vectors in the economy car market are completely different than those in the luxury automobile market or the pick-up truck market. You need to pick the right vectors that matter to your compact/luxury/truck customers or your ERP/CRM customers.

Most analysts try to distill markets into two vector grids, but markets and segments may have more than two vectors. There may be three or four or 42. This can make visualizing your market tough, but it is better to do the extra work and suffer the headaches of complete market positioning than to miss important elements. The point is that you must identify those vectors that matter and measure against them (and if they cannot be measured, then they are not viable vectors).

Also know that positioning can be different for every segment and the vectors are likely different for each segment (yes, positioning can get that tedious). Enjoy if you can this painful realization — that the work of segmenting never stops and that you must constantly review and refine you positioning. The routine nature of positioning analysis is another reason why marketing is a *discipline* in many senses of the word.

Here is a quick example of a positioning map Silicon Strategies Marketing created for a client in the software application development platform space (and this was a fairly long time ago, so the positions of these products are likely different today). In this map we identified two primary vectors on which to model the market, those being the number of software developers within a team or an entire organization, and the complexity of applications they created (and in this vector we merged missions criticality as a component of complexity). These two vectors were determined to be important from the customer's perspective — smaller organizations have different software development requirements and fewer governance restrictions than larger application development shops. Complexity is self-explanatory.

Positioning – an example

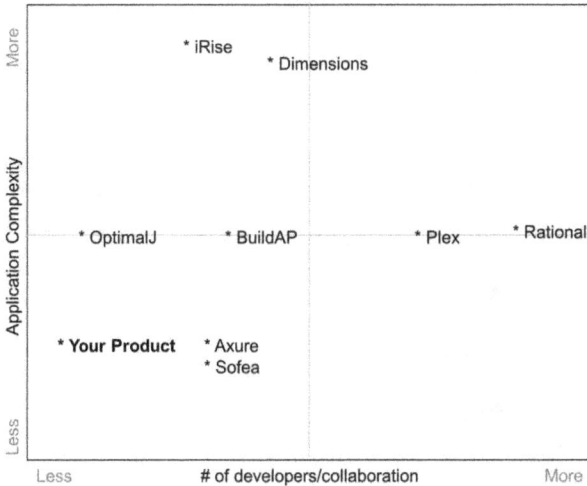

By mapping the competitors in the application development platform space, we saw that the product our client offered was ill-suited for either large and highly regulated development teams, or for intensely complex and mission-critical applications. Oddly, our client had originally planned on selling to customers in the upper-right quadrant. Avoiding that strategy saved them from a market disaster and wasting a large amount of marketing budget.

Most companies will only have two or three common positioning vectors. The graph to the right, done for another Silicon Strategies Marketing client, charted their three critical positioning vectors using the size of X-Y points for the third vector. It is nearly impossible to visualize more than three vectors in a positioning matrix. Thankfully, key buyer genotypes rarely have more than three *critical* issues in any segment.

Positioning – another example

Market Positioning

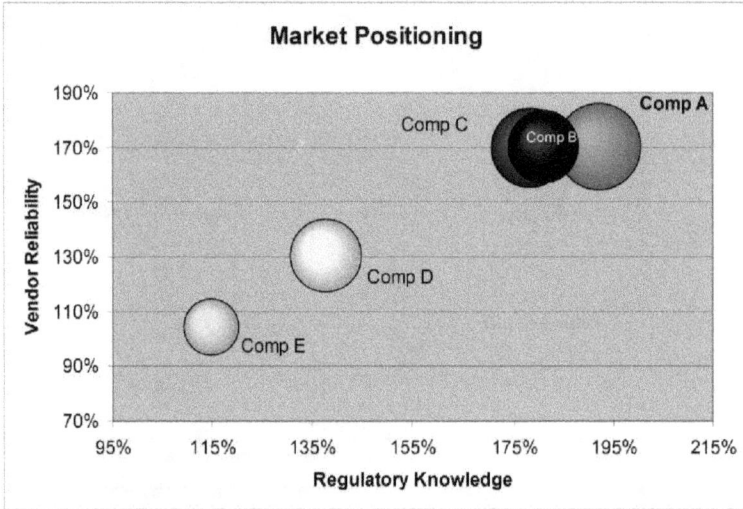

Your current position though is only the start of a long story. A common sin among young start-up companies is not only thinking unrealistically about where in the market they are today, but failing to think ahead about where they *want* to be next year and the year after that. Planning is an executive task, and not planning your next position is failing to do your planning.

Smart companies look at segments, mapping a progression plan that is both opportunistic – growing into new segments based on their existing strengths – and strategically focused on long-term game plans that bring them incrementally closer to providing a whole product for the entire market (or at least as close as is humanly possible). They also choose segments and feature combinations that move their position *around* those of their competitors, avoiding toe-to-toe competition. As my martial arts instructor was fond of saying, the fight you avoid is the fight you win.

You will develop market-wide whole products by **creating a series of segment whole products**. You do this to establish dominance and ensure cash flow. Any other approach is a get-rich-quick scheme, and we know how those typically turn out. The good news is that replotting your positioning as you enter new segments is an annual event, or one triggered by market-changing situations. It also isn't difficult if you have a suitably complete segmentation strategy and competitive analysis. Lacking either of those makes positioning exercises useless.

Positioning – changes over time

- Knowing where you are today is essential in mapping competitive threats and pressures
- It also provides a guidepost to where you can easily move next
- The primary path is toward the whole product definition and around competitors' strong positions

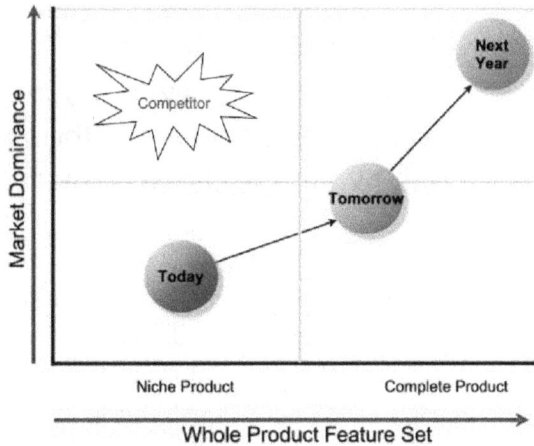

Market Dominance

Competitor

Next Year

Tomorrow

Today

Niche Product   Complete Product

Whole Product Feature Set

Central to establishing your positioning map and strategy is determining the relevant vectors for your market or segment. This is not as simple as some industry analyst groups maintain. The motivations of buyers in any given *market* are different, as are the breadth of customers. Multiply this by the number of segments and the problem grows geometrically. As an example, for many software suites in relatively mature markets the size of the customer – in terms of number of employees – is often a positioning vector. But for a product that only serves the SMB market, it may not be a relevant at all.

Positioning – determining the vectors

- **Mature markets**
  - Review competitors
  - Consult analysts
  - Evaluate prospect issues/goals
  - Look for common threads between all
- **New, post-chasm markets**
  - If the market is new enough, the established non-product solution is the primary (perhaps only) vector and competitor

---

If your market is anywhere past the chasm phase, then there is already a large pool of data that will help identify the relevant positioning vectors. Your competitors – whether they know it or not – may have listed important clues about positioning vectors on their websites. For example, one of the competitors shown in a previous chart said that the number of stakeholders outside of the software development organization was a key criterion in product selection. This information was in plain sight on their site, right on the product feature page. Someone in their marketing department got sloppy while writing copy.

Let's get back to analysts groups – the IDCs, Gartners and Forresters of the world. Analyst reports will often supply positioning vectors, but be careful. Analyst groups tend to create rather generic and market-wide positioning matrixes that ignore the customer perspective, which is all-important. They make money from both vendors and consumers, and thus have to communicate at the highest possible level. See what analysts say, but add your home-grown set of positioning elements. Never take gospel even from the analyst clergy.

In identifying potential positioning vectors, what you hear from prospects (not customers) may be the most important. When you listen and list their expected outcomes, you will detect common vectors. For example, if most of your prospects have an expected outcome of increasing sales closure rates, then that will lead you to a core positioning vector. The outcome isn't the vector, but the degree to which faster closing rates is business-critical is a positioning vector.

New markets make finding positioning vectors difficult. These markets are, by definition, ill-defined. What early adopters value is not what *the market* or even your beachhead segment value. The same rule about prospects applies to new markets and gives you early guidance, but you have to talk to people in the early majority phase of the market, even if the market has not reached that phase. A truly innovative product tends to define or redefine a market. Knowing which of those things your product is doing helps to identify the positioning vectors and who to talk to. Redefining a market means you may need to pick and discard various existing vectors while identifying new ones. Creating a new market or segment means you can only talk to early adopters and you might find that you have a one-vector positioning chart. This can be a legitimate positioning matrix (or should I say, *array*) for new markets.

Positioning – appropriate vectors

- ## Selecting vectors
    - Functional (whole product)
    - Symbolic (genotype motivations)
    - Complexity (scope across segments/markets)
    - Financial (TCO, capital vs. operational, etc.)

When positioning, there is no more important concept than picking the most appropriate vectors. You will likely identify many *possible* vectors, but some are not relevant, and others lack significant importance as far as customers are concerned. Vectors are the rational and appropriate dimensions on which all solutions available to the customer can be compared. Determining what is *rational* and *appropriate* is where most entrepreneurs go wrong when positioning their products. Founders allow their product vision (and thus their preconceived vectors) to bias their assessments. It is important to get outside views and choose vectors that are appropriate for your market and your segments as your prospects perceive it.

Vectors can be anything, but fall into one of a few categories. They can be **functional** vectors, based on the features that comprise the potential whole product for a market or segment. They can be **symbolic** vectors, relating to the motivations and expected outcomes of buyers. Vectors can also be **complexity**-based, denoting their ability to serve buyers across many segments or even many markets. Vectors can always be **financial** in nature, and this vector becomes more prevalent as the solutions in a market become commoditized.

One piece of advice: Positioning need not be engineering-level accurate. Using our Manhattan map analogy from earlier in this book, when positioning you do not *need* to know at what street number you and your competitors live. Typically you need to know which neighborhood you are in – are you in Marble Hill or Greenwich Village? Is your competitor in Turtle Bay or did they leave and take up residence out in Newark? Like any other topic, positioning can be over-analyzed, and modern markets move too fast for that luxury.

Market definition - SWOT

- SWOT – Strengths, Weaknesses, Opportunities, Threats
- SWOT analysis can and should be performed on the addressable market
- A separate SWOT analysis can and should be done for
  - Each segment you might enter
  - Against each competitor

Though not a positioning process per se, SWOT analysis leads to greater competitive understanding and often reveals relevant positioning vectors. SWOT stands for Strengths, Weaknesses, Opportunities and Threats. It is one of the classic evaluations of products within a market or segment. When building a SWOT analysis for your market and against each competitor, you will rapidly discover where lay your most significant problems. Where you find divergence between products is often where relevant vectors reside.

The elements in SWOT are:

Strengths are where you or a competitor have power in the market. It can be better features, more cash, better brand recognition, etc.

Weaknesses naturally are places where there is an inherent problem with a product or company. The same areas apply – features, money, momentum, etc.

Opportunities are the most interesting aspect of SWOT. These are places where a competitor can gain market share through untapped or under-exploited elements with little or no extra resources. Anticipating your and your competitors' opportunities may well tell you what next year's positioning map will look like.

Threats are elements that could do damage to your position in the market. These can be non-competitive things like government regulations, legal problems, patent disputes, and more. It can also be a major new release of a competing product, a new Open Source alternative, etc.

I have often summarized SWOT as:

> What are we/they good at?
> What needs fixing?
> Where is the next striking point?
> What do we need to watch out for?

If you are a start-up, having a solid SWOT analysis in your funding pitch is a demonstration to venture capitalists that you have done your homework on the market. It is the minimum degree of sophistication they expect. Do it.

SWOT analysis can be very complex. Here is an example of a *preliminary* SWOT Silicon Strategies Marketing did for a client long ago (the analysis may not hold-up today after all the competitors and their markets changed). In this study we settled for a high-level review of major product features, though there can be other factors included in a SWOT analysis.

Market definition – SWOT example

⊞ *High-level SWOT*

	Strength	Weakness	Opportunity	Threat
Axure	• Single purpose • Simple to use • "Reasonably" priced • Established traction • Workflows and component details • AJAX enabled	• No ARAD, no final application built • HTML prototyping only • Some negative reviews • No real data integration for simulation	• Limited scope (application animation) limits Axure market • They cannot deliver a final end-user application	• Fair mindshare for UI specialists and application designers • Could "price discount" against Brainwave
iRise	• Relatively complete (analysis through Q&A) • Gorilla with market share and financial strength • Good marketing and presentation of capabilities • Group collaboration features	• Expensive • Major commitment across teams and organization • Significant IT staff learning commitment • No final application built • No component or behavior mapping	• Over-reaching product scope allows for smaller and more agile tools • Final application delivery better for stand-alone and user specific application generation	• Collaboration blocks Brainwave from team-developer accounts
Serena	• Broad prototyping feature set • Huge revenue base creates powerful enhancement capabilities • Large installed base - unshakable • Change and release management helps meet regulations	• Most expensive competitor • Complex solution set with poor selling proposition • No final application delivery • Much of their offering are requirements database management	• Final application delivery better for stand-alone and user specific application generation	• Collaboration blocks Brainwave from team-developer accounts • Huge cash flow allows for fast reaction and extending product reach
Sofea	• Automatic test script generation a fairly unique feature	• Week product presentation • Weak ARAD and no	• Final application delivery better for stand-alone and user	• Improving their outbound market presentation wil

The key to SWOT is to evaluate strengths, weaknesses, opportunities and threats *based on market demands* and not your preconceptions of what makes a good product. The exception is when you are innovating a market and your offering creates fundamentally new opportunities against competitors. Great innovation creates solutions for problems people don't know they have, or accelerates their advantages in way they could not previously imagine (I always think of the first housewife to see the first washing machine, and who likely fainted on the spot).

Your Action List

1. Discover your market's meaningful positioning vectors and make sure they can be quantified.
2. Study both the reality and perception of every
   competitor against each vector.
3. Plot your current position in your current target segments and make changes to secure
   those segments.
4. Plot your position in your next target segments and plan changes to secure those.

Chapter 6 – Branding

> "Branding is <u>making</u> the market <u>think</u> and <u>feel</u> what you want them to about you and your products."©

Read the statement above over and over and over again. Memorize it. It is the most concise and realistic definition of branding ever written (penned by yours truly). Knowing, breathing and dreaming this definition will save you years of angst and a fair amount of heartburn.

Your brand is what the market thinks and feels about you and your products. Your job is to make the market think and feel what you want them to think and feel. Most start-ups don't, and in the absence of guidance, the market goes on to define the brand for them.

Let's break this down. People – individually and in the aggregate – think and they feel. These are different and interrelated aspects of being human. Ever meet someone who was obviously intelligent and well-studied, but you felt they were an idiot because of their beliefs? You *thought* one thing about this person – that they were smart – but *felt* exactly the opposite. Brands work the same way. We'll talk about this duality more in a moment. For now, read the definition of branding a few hundred more times until you know it as well as you know your own name.

Branding is the creation of an idea, then communicating it. You communicate to the market the essence of your company and your products that you want buyers to believe. It is this encapsulation of everything about a product that creates the foundation of belief about the product. The essence of a Porsche is vastly different than of a Fisker Karma, aside from the fact that one breaks down often while the other melts-down just as often. The *essence* of what a product is can drive an entire product line or even an entire corporation.

Branding – communicating essence

- Branding is a form of communicating
- Branding communicates the essence of the company or product
- Branding is the foundation statement about the value the customer receives
- BMW: The Ultimate Driving Machine
  - Never mentions automobiles
  - Communicates driving (an act), machines (male-centric concept) and ultimate (nothing better)
  - The BMW brand claims they will bring to you the best experience in a thrilling activity through the best engineering possible

---

BMW is a study of effective branding whereby they make buyers both think and feel specific things about BMW automobiles. Take their slogan – The Ultimate Driving Machine. Analyze that in terms of what it makes you think and feel about their product:

Ultimate: Describes a pinnacle of achievement.

Driving: Not an object but an event, an experience.

Machine: Denotes precision and power.

In three words BMW tells buyers that they will achieve the peak experience possible commanding powerful machinery to heighten the already enjoyable sensation of driving (unless you and your BMW get stuck behind a broken Porsche or get hit by an exploding Ford).

Branding - foundation

- Knowing your buyer genotypes and their motivations
- Knowing what your organization and products actually mean
- Finding the intersection between what you are and what buyers want
- Foreshadowing where you need to be next

In order to select your brand, you need to construct a foundation based in large part on your target buyers and their motivations. This foundation should first match who your organization actually is and what your products really deliver. Where the two agree – market motivations and your actual strengths – is where your brand strength lies. They do not need to be exact matches, but they better be close neighbors. Stretch a brand too far and it breaks.

Once you have found the important intersections between what the market wants and what you can deliver, incorporate as many emotional modifiers and amplifiers as possible. Remember that emotive promotions outperform rational ones. Remember too that your brand is designed to make people feel as well as think. Getting strong emotions (e.g., ultimate experience) attached to your functional value ignites both halves of the brain and creates a complete perception (head and gut) about your company and product.

In crafting a brand, you _**must**_ speak to both the logical and emotional sides of the brain – the left and the right, if you will. Think about a car advertisement that lists its horsepower and miles per gallon. Now picture the same ad with a slinky blonde draped across the hood and a suggestive headline. Same car. Same horsepower. Same mileage. Different brand because now you feel. You emote. You have a slavishly emotional connection between the object and an expected outcome.

Selling technology is exactly the same. Apple did not make the first MP3 player, nor at the time the best one available. But they knew how to attach the device to the emotional desire to feel joyful while listening to music. As you saw earlier, I did the same with IT utility software and won a 26% sales bump by doing so. Never fear appealing to human emotion — just be sure you select the right emotions and that they are not objectionable to potential buyers. Slinky blondes in revealing gowns will not sell many rosary beads.

Branding – why emotions matter in B2B

- Everyone is a human
- Everyone has egocentric motivations
- Conflicts and personal objectives color corporate objectives
- Corporate realities shape personal fears
- A vendor that taps into the emotive side of a buy decision will beat a competitor that does not

I'm a PC.   I'm a Mac.

"A great brand taps into emotions. Emotions drive most, if not all, of our decisions. A brand reaches out with a powerful connecting experience. It's an emotional connecting point that transcends the product."

- Scott Bedbury/Nike, Starbucks

Everyone is human (your congressman may be the exception). Everyone has motivations attached to their ego. Often there are conflicts between the individual motivation and the corporate objective. But there are overlaps between the two as well. Any time you find compatibility between emotive, personal objectives of genotypes and the needs of the organization they serve, then you have a fast path to closing a deal – the individual is gratified and the bureaucracy will not object. The inverse however is deadly. Choose a brand that runs contrary to organizational culture and you will doom sales before your account executives ever pick-up the phone.

This advantage cannot be dismissed. Let's say you and your competitor have reasonably identical products in terms of functional outcomes. But assume your competitors only promote their features and functions, while you do that and appeal to some emotional element common to your key buyer genotypes – their hopes, dreams, nightmares. You will win the sale because the buyer has an emotional connection with your product – they *believe* instead of merely *think*.

Scott Bedbury – the fellow who guided Nike and Starbuck brands – believes the same thing, even though Silicon Strategies Marketing defined the term branding better than Scott. *"Just Do It!"* sold the essence of authentic athletic achievement, but it never sold shoes. Shoes were secondary to the emotional desire to excel. Nike promoting athleticism and Apple promoting musical joy show clearly how emotions drive brand bias. There is nothing better than to have buyers biased toward what you sell.

Branding – what it is *not*

- It is not
  - a logo
  - a letter head
  - an advertising campaign
- Your brand is the essence (primarily real) of your company and products
- Brand essence is communicated in part through logos, advertising, letterheads

---

An important side note here. You will encounter a large set of charlatans – masquerading as consultants – who think *branding* is art work. They pitch to you that branding is a logo, a color scheme and website design. This is so wrong that anyone selling such branding services should be shown the door ... to an open elevator shaft. Colors, logos and indeed everything your customers encounter about your company should reflect the brand you define, what you want them to think and feel about you. If your brand is defined in part as being warm and intimate, mellow earth tones are in order. If your brand is solid and professional, then corporate mahogany and maroon may work. Your goal, your job, is to define your brand and then select graphics that communicate your stated brand, not the other way around.

You can also augment your basic brand statement with elements that hint at your next planned market position. Recall that buyers in your next target segment are often the early adopters of that segment. You can extend your brand in order to attract customers in your currently prioritized segment as well as encouraging investigation of buyers in the next segment. Since these segments are closely related it may be easy.

Everything from your website to how your receptionist answers the phone should reflect your brand. Since branding facilitates customer acceptance and sales, getting branding right and driving it throughout your entire organization is one of your primary jobs. Any place where your customers encounter your company or your product is a branding touch point, right down to the graphic icons in your user interface. A CEO's job is to get everyone in an organization on the same page. Assuring that everyone in your organization knows, believes and projects your brand is your responsibility.

The first step is to clearly define your brand. If you cannot put your brand in writing, you cannot hope to describe it to your employees much less your customers.

Once your brand is defined in a clear, concise statement, you communicate it throughout the organization and at every possible opportunity. Fred Smith, the founder of FedEx, constantly repeats the FedEx mission, for their "team members to keep focused on delivering an **outstanding FedEx experience** to our customers and to each other." Back when they were a healthy and growing retailer, Circuit City was all about customer service and it was preached from the CEO, through all executives and in the house organ.

You will eventually need to measure how the market perceives your brand. You want to know where the market's perception and your brand statements disagree. Small exceptions are not fatal and typically cured over time and with PR diligence (which in modern times includes a healthy amount of social media work). Larger gaps indicate a significant problem. Typically this involves start-up founders defining an unrealistic brand or one that does not match their true product and corporate culture. It is rarely a defect in market perception. Keep in mind that the market ultimately decides your brand. It is up to you to guide their decision. In the absence of your guidance, the market will write your brand statement for you, and it is rarely complementary.

A case in point: When Silicon Strategies Marketing started advising SuSE Linux on their North American marketing strategy around the millennial cusp, the market's perception of SuSE was "small, quirky, German Linux distro." SuSE had never internally defined their brand, much less tried to communicate any concise brand to the market. In the absence of real branding effort, the market composed SuSE's brand based on whatever disinformation they heard. The market's brand definition for SuSE was unflattering for a product being peddled to CIOs and CTOs. We redefined the SuSE brand in North America as "the Linux designed for enterprise infrastructure", and then promoted SuSE differentiation that matched long-term CxO strategy. In other words, we crafted a brand specifically for our target genotype.

When you and your team sit to define your brand, keep in mind that there are limits to brands. If you try to go beyond these limits, your brand will fail and be ridiculed by the market. You may remember when Microsoft hired Jerry Seinfeld to make Microsoft look cool. The "cool" brand image went too far beyond what the market believed about Microsoft since there is nobody less cool than Bill Gates. Microsoft's effort was widely ridiculed.

Your brand must be anchored in reality – your reality and your customers' reality. It needs to closely match what you, your company and your products deliver, and it cannot stray too far from what the market is willing to believe. You need to understand the realistic boundaries of your products and the worldview of your target genotypes. Your brand must reflect a true essence of the product within the tolerance of buyers.

Branding – reality and fakery

- Brands must be real
- Brands must reflect a true essence
- If a brand lies, the brand dies
- It is okay to have a brand that is slightly exaggerated, but never patently false
- If your brand scope grows too large, you may be forced into maintaining multiple brands
  - Brand elasticity has limits – one size does not fit all

If your brand lies, it dies.

If your brand makes promises but fails to deliver, the market will rewrite your brand, and the market's rebranding will be so negative that it might singularly kill your company. When SCO sued IBM and Novell, everyone remotely associated with the Linux market reassigned the SCO brand to that of lawyer-loving litigious pinheads, and not a software company. SCO died a slow, miserable and painful death.

Brands *can* be exaggerated … to a limit. It is okay to exaggerate your brand, but only a little. The market is not unwise to marketing hype and they will tolerate a little excess. They will not tolerate outright deception. Exaggerating your brand in the direction you intend to move your product can actually have long-term benefits providing you enhance your product quickly.

Finally, all brands have a different amount of **brand elasticity**, which we will define as the ability to stretch the perception of the product or company. Apple has been able to stretch their brand from computers for the art community to hip consumer entertainment devices. But Apple has never been able to stretch their brand to be a serious IT alternative, despite having arguably higher quality and stability than many alternatives. Be conscious of this last example because this shows clearly where different market segments have different criteria and reject any product or brand that does not closely agree with their perceptions.

Branding – maintaining multiple brands

- Proctor and Gamble
- Over 100 different brands
- Two categories – laundry detergent and fabric softeners
- Each brand has a different position, price value proposition and market segment

cheer (color guard)   **Bounce**

Dreft   Downy

ERA   **Tide**

GAIN

If you find your brand being stretched too far or in too many directions, your brand will eventually break. Sometimes it makes more sense to have multiple brands than to risk rupturing one. Take Proctor and Gamble. They have over 100 different brands, many of which compete with one another. An example is laundry detergent. The Tide brand could not successfully be stretched to simultaneously be all-purpose, spring-fresh, and color-protecting. So P&G makes different products that sell these different perceived benefits and thus represent different brands. They all achieve the one basic function of laundry detergent, namely to clean your clothing, but each brand caters to a different market segment with different brand preferences.

Banding – make it concise

- ## Define it in 20 words or less
  - Nike = Authentic athletic performance
  - Starbucks = A great coffee experience
  - BMW = The ultimate driving machine
  - Rubric = A better localization experience
  - Microsoft = You will be assimilated

In a perfect world you are able to distill your brand into a tag line, a slogan. You may not be able to do this with *your* brand, but your goal is to be as concise as possible. A brand statement with lots of words creates confusion or ambiguity. So distill, distill, and distill until you have a compelling and precise statement of your brand. Few companies strive for this, but the ones that do have great brand equity and do a lot of business.

And most of all remember that your primary job vis-à-vis branding is to communicate it *through* your employees. The simpler and more precise the brand statement, the easier it is to remember, repeat and believe.

There are a number of rather esoteric sounding terms bandied about by branding experts. As fanciful as they sound, they are important concepts that you need to understand. It pays to know what your marketing team and your outside agencies are talking about.

Brand awareness is simple – it is a measure of if the market knows your brand and how well they know it. Those are different metrics. A large number of people know that U.S. Steel exists but very few people know what their brand is ("Making steel, building value, world competitive").

• Brand awareness	• Do I know you?
• Brand strength	• Can I believe you?
• Brand elasticity	• Are you too big?
• Brand equity	• Are you valuable?

Brand strength is the measure of how thoroughly the market *believes* your stated brand. If you are Apple, the market believes every word Steve Jobs used to say. If you are Microsoft, they take your brand with several sacks of salt.

Brand elasticity we already covered, but to repeat, it is how far you can extend your brand to cover multiple products, segments or markets. Apple's brand spans iPods and iPhones, but starts to break down at enterprise servers.

Brand equity describes how valuable a brand is to the customer. The brand equity of BMW is very different than the brand equity for Suzuki.

Customers go through several stages as they adopt brands. Having an idea of the typical stages of brand adoption and how long your product or company has been at any one stage tells you much about your products and where they stand in the mind of buyers compared to alternatives. It also shows that you must lead customers through each of these stages (Apple seems to be very good at taking the market from awareness to religion in a single step).

First, people have to be **aware** that you even exist (brand awareness). This is why advertising still has a place in product marketing. You need to make people aware that you are even alive before they can know what you offer.

Next, they have to have some **knowledge** of your brand – what it stands for as well as what your products do. Many of the dot-com spendthrifts thought hip brand awareness was all they needed and thus drove their start-ups into the peat.

Branding – the brand adoption hierarchy

- ## Where are you in the customer brand adoption process?
  - Brand awareness
  - Brand knowledge
  - Brand acceptance
  - Brand preference
  - Brand loyalty
  - Brand avocation
  - Brand religion

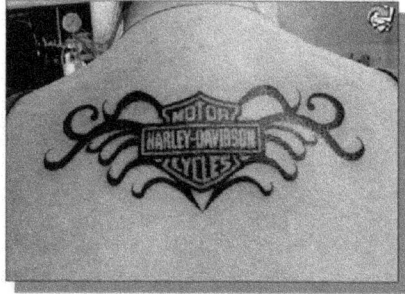

The market then needs to **accept** your brand promise even if it is merely a tentative acceptance. Acceptance is a critical phase. Ever turn down a pushy sales person? You instinctively didn't accept his brand promise. However, if you stopped to look at a product on a shelf, having seen a television advertisement, you subconsciously were mulling over the brand promise to decide if you should test it. This is a tentative buy-in state and one necessary before mass adoption is possible (I'll note in passing that online content products have an easier time than other products because of the ease of branding and the ability of customers to sample and share it if the brand promise has been satisfied).

After customers have some experience with your and other brands, and when you consistently prove your brand's promise, customers may start to develop a **preference** for your brand. All other things being equal, they will choose your brand– but *only* when all other things are equal. Your competitor's job is to make things unequal.

When consistently pleased, when you routinely deliver more than the customer expects, customers go beyond mere preference. They become **loyal** (brand loyalty), refusing to even consider alternatives. In the absence of something significantly better, your customers simply don't care about switching. Remember WebCrawler? They were the preferred Web search engine with significant customer loyalty until Google made something significantly better.

Branding – loyalty

- ## Branding builds loyalty
  - Loyalty pays
    - "Loyalty leaders" earn 12% higher profits
    - "Loyalty laggards" earn 11% less
  - Coca Cola as an example
    - Over $46 billion in "customer good will"
- ## Branding builds believability and desire
  - What better way to motivate new customers

One step beyond loyalty is **avocation**, where customers begin bragging about your products to other people. When you achieve this level of brand stickiness, sales occur automatically and your competitors struggle to stay alive. Achieving brand avocation is about as far as most marketers can hope to rise.

The pinnacle is brand **religion**, where the customer adopts your brand as part of their lifestyle, their very being. Harley Davidson owners have brand religion. So do Oakland Raider fans. When customers tattoo your logo on their butts, you have achieved brand religion.

This attachment to a brand is important because it is free money. One study (Walker Information IT Survey, 2004) indicated that companies that maintain high brand loyalty earn 12% higher profits than average, while brand laggards make 11% less. Band religion pays a 23% premium.

In fact, your accountant tracks the value of your brand. On corporate balance sheets, "customer good will" is a charge that roughly reflects the *lifetime* brand equity earned. Coca Cola is one of the strongest brands on the planet and they have (last time I looked) over $46 billion in customer good will. They earned it over decades and through very good marketing practices, nurturing the Coca Cola brand one polar bear at a time.

But most important, branding builds **believability** and **desire** in the hearts of customers. When people went into Best Buy in the early days of the iPod, they wanted iPods. Not what Creative Labs sold, or Sony sold, or anyone else sold. Apple created in the souls of music lovers the **belief** that iPods would make them happier people, and thus the desire to own an iPod. Nothing else would do. From that seed their brand extended to iPhones, iPads and next year, iSpouse (sadly the female edition of the iSpouse looks like Steve Wozniak).

The point behind branding is that when done well, you create an unfair advantage in the market. Great branding biases purchasing decisions before the customer engages with the product, even when new products come into your market or when the market changes. This unfair advantage will not only earn you revenues, it will befuddle your competitors. A weak product with a great brand will do better than a strong product with a weak brand.

Here is a positive branding case study. Rubric was a Silicon Strategies Marketing client. They are in the language services business and help software companies make their products ready for foreign markets. Their target genotype is executives in multi-national companies.

After conducting deep interviews (a qualitative market research process) with target genotypes and noting their motivations, we drafted a brand statement for Rubric — one that reflected both the functional and emotional motivations of their buyers and motivations that their competitors had ignored. We then amplified the basic brand statement to express what we wanted the market to *think* and *feel* about Rubric.

Once written this way, Rubric could achieve two things. First, We gave Rubric's executives talking points and phrases to use while communicating internally to their staffs in the U.K., United States, Asia and other locations – this assured that Rubric troops constantly understood the brand's objective and took appropriate actions to make customers feel that brand.

Branding – a quick example

- **Company**: Rubric
- **Product**: Language services
- **Customers**: Executives in multi-national companies
- **Brand**: You can trust Rubric's on-demand globalization services to make your products a success.
  - **Think**: Rubric is a safe bet – they will deliver accurate localizations thanks to excellent project management, on-demand scalability and corporate-wide integrity.
  - **Feel**: Safety and confidence because Rubric's processes and track record will keep you from being a failure.

Second, these raw statements were given to the designer responsible for the website and collateral, and to any writer creating marketing copy. We asked each of them to print the brand statement out and tape it above their computer monitors, check their work to assure it reflected the brand.

The net effect is that the brand is constantly and consistently echoed in every communication to every prospect and customer. Prospects soon started echoing the brand back to Rubric. Sales resistance (in their highly cost-competitive market) dropped. Rubric did what every good company should – they defined their brand and lived it daily. Their business actually *grew* during the 2009 recession when many competitors suffered.

Have a look at how the brand statement influenced the design of the Rubric website. The designer's first layout used traditional corporate tones that said, "We are a solid company," which conveyed the "trust" aspect of the brand. In their industry filled with many small, fragile and operationally inadequate competitors, this was an important element of the brand. The designer used images that showed themes that echoed "international" and "multi-cultural." Throughout we used customer quotes to confirm the core message that Rubric was a wise choice – that choosing them was a safe bet and a better localization experience.

To this day it remains the focus of that company.

Now here is a good example of bad branding, and one shamefully enough created by J. Walter Thompson's German division at the insistence of SuSE Linux's German office marketing chief. While Silicon Strategies Marketing was creating SuSE Linux's North American brand, SuSE's VP of marketing in Germany asked JWT to make the SuSE brand "irreverent."

Branding – a bad example

- JWT developed an "irreverent" campaign for SuSE Linux
- Linux was positioned for mission-critical server application support
- SuSE's brand needed to reinforce their commitment to Linux, enterprises, IBM and serious business computing
- JWT's campaign violated the brand essence

Yeah, I didn't get that either.

JWT should have turned them down. Good consultants avoid damaging their customers. SuSE sold IT infrastructure software to chief technology officers – people whose technology decisions affect the fate of their companies for years to come. Irreverence was the opposite of what CTOs wanted from an operating system vendor. Instead, SuSE needed to create and reinforce a brand that had started to grow organically due to their association with IBM – namely one that matched the level of seriousness enterprise CTOs and CIOs had about mission-critical infrastructure. Indeed, even before the IBM association and SuSE's growth in North America, SuSE had earned among techies a brand of "oddball Linux company with bullet-proof products." Thus the direction from the German office and JWT's ad concepts not only violated SuSE's actual and growing organic brand, they violated the desired brand.

Incidentally, the VP of marketing was not retained by Novell after the acquisition.

Again, branding is conceptually simple, but you must define your brand and communicate it through every corner of your organization and your market. Do not leave this to chance.

Your Action List

1. Define what you want the market to *think* and *feel* about your products and your company.
2. Make sure the brand is real.
3. Compose internal brand statements that help your employees communicate the brand every time.
4. Guide buyers through each phase of brand attachment.
5. Communicate your brand relentlessly via your employees and marketing.

Chapter 7 – Messaging

Messaging is **_not_** self-explanatory.

A message is conceptually simple. It is the transfer of a concept from one person to another. However, there are planned messages, unplanned messages, well-targeted messages, poorly targeted messages and accidental messages. If you do not catalogue the motivations of your buyer genotypes and if you do not anticipate their concerns and objections, your messages will not move them to buy your products and may instead create barriers to sales.

The simple approach to messaging – which I will make vastly more complicated as we go – is to think like a news reporter, and ask yourself who, what, how and when.

> **Who** am I communicating to and why do they care?
>
> **What** do they need and want to hear about?
>
> **How** do they prefer to learn what I have to tell them?
>
> **When** is the communication occurring and how does that affect the message?

What you will rapidly discover is that mapping all of your messages cannot be done in just two dimensions, though I bet you have tried once or twice to do so. This is where many start-ups go wrong. They try to cobble together messages that appeal broadly to multiple audiences in many venues and media, and during all phases of the sales cycle.

That doesn't work. One-size-fits-all pantyhose never do.

Think for a moment about all the different types of people you need to communicate to – the consumers of your messages – and how different are their motivations. Customers and industry analysts look at products from opposite ends of the spectrum – from a buy decision to a market-mapping analysis. Investors want to know how the product will make them rich while the media wants to see a good story they can tell. If you create only one message and take it to each of these groups, all of the groups will be disappointed.

Messaging – messy

- **Try drawing a matrix for all combinations**
  - Who
    - Customers
    - Media
    - Analysts
    - Investors
  - Where
    - Several markets segments, genotypes
    - Web, magazine, trade shows
  - When
    - Initial engagement
    - Deeper investigation
    - Objection to offer
    - Closing the deal

The same complication applies to *where* your messages appear, but more importantly *when* they appear. Your messaging should be different at all points in the technology adoption lifecycle (the macro view) as well as every phase of a sale (micro view). Taking time to map out your messages and to tweak them as you test those messages in the market is a small investment compared to the wasted time and brand destruction resulting from having sloppy messages.

There is a hierarchy and order of messages you will develop. Each group of messages are the seeds for other messages, and it is important to tackle messages in a specific order.

Core messages are, as the name suggests, the central messages and key value propositions that every possible audience receives about your products. Though complete messaging is different for each genotype, the kernel of the messaging should be consistent across the entire market and all receivers. Since common motivators are few for all these different audiences, the core messages must be limited to your top value propositions and differentiators.

Field messages are those used in the field, typically for sales efforts. In the age of the Internet, a field message may be on a website or it may be in a specific piece of collateral a prospect is automatically emailed late in the sales cycle. If they are used in any *specific* sales phase, they are a field message.

Messages need to be tailored to specific **genotypes**. Thus a set of field messages in the third phase of your sales cycle may be different for each genotype that influences the sales decision. Yes, complex sales into enterprises require a lot of messaging to a lot of different people, and the message manual can get thick.

Likewise, messages may differ for each **segment** in your market. After all, segments exist because the *needs* for each segment are different. Genotypes, motivations, value propositions and thus field messages will change between segments. The astute reader realizes that in a field marketing message there may exist a 3D message matrix, combining segment, genotype and sales phase. You are right and it is common for top-tier vendors to document each of the cells in the matrix.

Finally, there are special case messages that need to be developed for special situations or events. Politicians caught with interns in motel rooms often have to create such messages.

It's time to go deeper in the messaging mire. Let's start with core market messages, which are the seeds for all other messages that you or your teams will write. Keep in mind that core messages change as products, markets and competitors change. Nothing lasts forever. When your seed messages change, you have to review and revise all the messages that are built on top of them.

Messaging – the fundamental types

- ## Core messages
  - – Seeds for all other messages
- ## Field messages
  - – Messages for engaging customers at all phases of the sales cycle
- ## Genotype-specific messages
  - – Variation of core and field messages appropriate for different influencers
- ## Segment-specific messages
  - – Variations on core messages for different segments
- ## Topic- or audience-specific messages
  - – Special messages for special situations

Core marketing messages are designed to capture the *core value proposition* of a product, a service or a company. If you ever see marketing materials where you cannot figure out what the value behind the product is, odds are the company never developed a set of core messages. You cannot hope to communicate to customers what you have not defined, and core market messages are the most basic definition of your product.

There are basically three key core marketing message types, and each is distilled from the one before it.

Messaging – core market messages

- "Seeds" for all other messages
- Designed to capture core value propositions of a product, service, company
- Three types
  - **Statement:** 2-5 paragraphs that communicate all the essential information, values and differentiations of the offering
  - **Blurb:** 1-2 paragraphs distilled from the statement and suitable for high-level overviews
  - **Elevator pitch:** Distilled from blurb and communicating the key value proposition in 30 seconds or less
- Tag lines are distilled elevator pitches (BMW)

The **statement** is longish text (3-5 paragraphs) that communicates all the essential information about the subject. "Statements" are rarely seen by customers. They are tools for communicating internally what your teams need to know about a product or your company.

Once a statement is written you distill from it a **blurb**, which is a one- or two-paragraph high-level description. Think of the blurbs you used to see in product guides, back when those were published and snail-mailed out to customers. A blurb is a highly condensed version of what you want the customer to know about you or your product without omitting any *critically important* element (non-critical elements should be disposed).

From your blurb you distill your **elevator pitch**, which is what you would say to a person in an elevator after they ask, "So, what is your product?" or "What does your company do?" Elevator pitches are short, 25 words max, and are designed to be delivered before the elevator stops and the other person gets off. The job of the elevator pitch is to cause the other passenger to stay on the elevator until it reaches your floor because they want to learn more from you. It is the push-up bra of marketing.

Note that the elevator pitch is indirectly distilled from your statement, but it has gone from two or more paragraphs down to less than 25 words. **_Do not_** try to distill your elevator pitch directly from the statement. Create the blurb and distill your elevator pitch from that. The blurb forces clear thinking about what can safely be removed and what absolutely must stay. BMW did not get down to "The Ultimate Driving Machine" by accident.

Messaging – creating core messages

- List motivations/outcomes for all genotypes across all active segments
- Find the common/similar motivations
- Weed out competitor strength points
- Compose product description
- Distill to Blurb
- Distill to elevator pitch
- Test, test, test

The path to creating your core marketing messages first involves listing all the motivations and expected outcomes for all your genotypes in all of your active and near-future segments. Remember always it is your customers' motivations that count, not your features.

Once they all have been written down, look for common motivations between all your segments and genotypes. You will not always find common motivations, but when they exist, they create the best anchors for your core marketing messages because they communicate key values to most or all of the people that influence the decision to buy your product.

Once you have documented all the common motivations, drop any that your competitors can legitimately claim or that are their top strengths. You need to show buyers why you are different, not the same as the other guy.

With what is left, write your statement, distill that into your blurb, and distill your blurb into an elevator pitch.

Once all this work is done, test your messages in a structured way that allows you to clearly see which messages and variations resonate with your buyers. There is no shame in getting your core messages wrong — only in keeping bad messages.

Messaging – creating core messages

Dept.	Genotype	Motivators	Demotivators
IT	CTO	• Architecting corporate-wide infrastructures that reduce mistakes and costs[26] • Reducing the number of technologies and unifying systems • Open standards-based technologies Diff-5,8: Brainwave's Open Source foundation and tight integration of standards-based frameworks is what makes Brainwave work so well.	• Non-standard products. My job is to standardize everything, including tools and processes. Don't break that. • Anything not based on open standards, if not actually open source Diff-5: Brainwave introduces no new technologies. We build upon open standards (web, AJAX, SOA, etc.) and Open Source (Python, etc.)[26] • Non-extensible, non-integratable products[27] • Scalability – apps tend to grow out of control and I am in charge of making sure things work well regardless of the number of users and don't lock us in or out[28] • We don't have time to learn yet another technology Diff-1,2,3,4,8: The learning curve for Brainwave is almost non-existent, and eliminates the need for specialized developer knowledge/skills (and cheaper too – you can hire low-skill developers)
IT	Application manager	• Meeting growing application demands • Getting more code written without more budget • High per/developer productivity Diff-1,2: Brainwave's unique database and integrated frameworks eliminate unnecessary and tedious application development tasks, and lets app programmers expedite development.	• Non-portable programming talent – need to keep team members using a small set of technologies[29] • Insecure methodologies – under governance pressure Diff-7: Capability-based security, designed from the beginning into every aspect of the Brainwave platform, enforce security-minded development. • Quality can't suffer

Here is an example of a preliminary core message framework that Silicon Strategies Marketing devised for a client. You can see how we listed for each genotype their motivators and demotivators, then color-coded them so we could find common motivations. Once that was done, we listed the product differentiators and tied them to these common motivators.

Note that last part carefully! Match what makes you different to what unites everyone who influences the decision to buy your product. Have a very clear picture of what the market is hungry for and how your product uniquely sates that hunger. If you can't find that combination, you may not have a viable product to offer.

Core message – Chasm alternative

Positioning Statement Template

- **For** *[target customer or market]*
- **Who have** *[compelling reason to buy]*,
- **Our company provides a** *[new / existing product category]*
- **That** *[key benefit addressing directly the compelling reason to buy]*.
- **Unlike** *[the reference or economic alternatives]*,
- **Our product** *[reflects a meaningful differentiation specifically related to an attribute(s) associated with the target audience]*.

The folks at the Chasm Group have a process for creating positioning statements, which as an end product is not too far removed from a blurb. If you are not a wordsmith and need to kick-start a message creation process, complete their fill-in-the-blank script — you may well end up with a serviceable blurb. If nothing else, do this as an in-house team-alignment exercise to help clarify and simplify your thinking.

Though we never used the Chasm script for our work at Telamon, this is a representation of how we might have applied it to the paging software I described earlier. Keep in mind this is not advertising copy — it is for your *internal* reference use so that you and your employees know who you are, what you sell and why buyers should care.

Core message – Chasm alternative applied

For enterprises who have automated systems or network monitoring suites, Telamon provides paging software that reliably and automatically locates and notifies support staff members unlike unwatched consoles. TelAlert creates peace of mind by eliminating the stress of manual monitoring and intervention by systems operators or help desk teams.

Now here is where the real pain starts.

When you have multiple genotypes and multiple segments and multiple products, messaging can get a little cumbersome. The good news

Messaging – the segment multiplier

	Segment #1	Segment #2	Segment #3	Segment #4	Segment #5
Genotype #1	1	2	3	4	5
Genotype #2	6	7	8	9	10
Genotype #3	11	12	13	14	15
Genotype #4	16	17	18	19	20

is, not all genotypes are important for all products or all segments, so many of the cells in a messaging matrix might be blank. But failing to account for all possible, relevant combinations or not discovering the motivations in each cell always means lackluster messaging and imprecise targeting, which results in disappointing sales and disappointed investors.

Messaging – field marketing messages

- Messages designed to be used "in the field" to move prospects into the next phase of the buying process
- Sales phases are dependent on:
  - The maturity of the market
  - The complexity and price of the product
  - The education of the prospect
- Field messages typically involve:
  - **Message:** what you say to move the sale forward
  - **Arguments:** anticipated reactions/objections
  - **Responses:** how to remove argument barriers

Let's talk a bit about field marketing messages. These are the messages your customers receive throughout the sales process. These include the messages they see on advertisements, in email webinar invitations, spoken during first sales calls, in product demos, contract negotiations, post-sales check-ups and even on your website if you have a well-thought-out funnel and chain of actions.

Sales efforts that start well can die if a sales person ad-libs late-phase field messages. You need to *understand and document your sales cycle* in order to understand the phases therein, and you must understand your sales cycles before composing field messages. Many common sales phase templates exist, and unless you are in a new, innovative industry or have very unusual customers, these common templates will often work well.

Sales phases – the different points in the customer's processes of discovery, education, evaluation, negotiation and purchase – are different for different products and markets primarily due to three factors. The first factor is the **maturity of the market**. Early markets are new, products are innovative or disruptive, and interested buyers need a lot of education to overcome their uncertainty. Thus you may have several more sales steps in your early market sales cycle than in a mature market where products are commodities, where branding, price and minor differentiators sway buyer decisions.

The product's **complexity** is also a factor that defines your sales phases. The more complex a product the more steps your customers will need and want to go through before making a decision and — not oddly — the more genotypes who will influence the decision.

How well educated your customer is on competitive market offerings will affect the number of sales phases. In the early days of high-definition television when the standards were new, prices were high and the buying public was not yet educated, the sales process was slow and often a customer made several trips to the store or to websites. The market is now well educated, prices are low and buy decisions are made with very little effort or resistance.

After you document your sales phases, you need to anticipate how to move each genotype from one phase to the next. Your messages are designed to remove buyer resistance in the current sales phase and lead them into the next (remember, make products easy to *buy via* removing friction/resistance). At each phase buyers have both spoken and unspoken arguments against buying. Thus, for each sales phase there is a dialogue where you provide motivating messages. The buyer then likely displays resistance by arguing or asking questions. You retaliate with more messages that remove or diminish their objections and thus reduce their reasons not to move forward to the next step, the next phase in the sales cycle.

It should be clear that you cannot anticipate each **message, argument** and **response** for every genotype in every segment for every product and all markets. But you can anticipate the common ones and document new ones as you encounter them. You can also test messages and responses and choose the ones that move buyers rapidly toward purchase decisions.

Keep in mind that every product and marketing strategy is different, which means every set of sales phases is different. Take the time to look at the phases encountered in your common and successful sales. Create a custom sales phase map for your products. You will want to map these sales phases to your CRM system's opportunity definitions and create your field message manual around each phase.

Let's look at some very common sales phases in enterprise technology sales. This model may not apply to your products and your markets, but it representative of common buying decision processes and helps you to understand sales phase modeling before executing your initial mapping efforts:

Messaging – field marketing messages

- ## Typical technology sales phases
  - **Initial contact:** what to tell the prospect when introducing a product
  - **Investigative questions:** what the prospect will likely want to learn about the product
  - **Solution recital:** responses that communicate value based on arguments/objections and individual needs
  - **Solution agreement:** tying the product to the customer need
  - **Closing:** eliminating any reason not to buy

Initial contact: The stage where the prospect has become aware that you exist.

Investigative: Once the prospect has decided they have a need (which was explained during the initial contact) and that your product might provide a suitable solution, buyers actively learn more while comparing alternatives.

Solution recital: Where you have engaged the prospect, learned more about their specific motivations/needs, answered their initial questions and are now specifying a solution set with a clear value proposition.

Solution agreement: Where the prospect has reviewed your recital and agrees that you have a potentially acceptable offering.

Closing: The final phase where you seek and get the contract, meeting final objections and negotiating price.

Messaging – field message example

Phase	Message	Arguments	Responses
Initial Contact	ZZZZZ eases your application backlog by eliminating development roadblocks. ZZZZZ improves your staff's requirements gathering, simplifies development, and makes maintenance pain free through a unified platform. Your developers are more productive and can now focus on the needs of the end-users, and not the minutia of the underlying technology. ZZZZZ data storage systems create and optimize the database directly from the application's design and logic. Together with our integrated frameworks and prepackaged tools, and ground-up security systems, application prototyping and development becomes a design function, not a technology trauma.	*RAD is the process of getting it wrong many times before getting it right once!*	Unlike RAD, ZZZZZ embraces the full development cycle including prototyping. ZZZZZ makes it easy for a developer to work alongside end-users to assure application requirements and business logic are captured correctly and approved from the beginning.
		Poorly designed applications are difficult to maintain, upgrade, and port. Why would I want to encourage a "design-on-the-fly" mentality?	ZZZZZ eliminates "design-on-the-fly" problems created by RAD systems. ZZZZZ allows prototypes to be created, remotely critiqued, and refined before committing. And even if there is a design defect, the intelligent neural database adapts to deign changes without tedious reengineering. This includes changes rolled onto production server.
		Isn't this just prototyping? I'll just have to redo this all over again and port it into our standard infrastructure.	The ZZZZZ platform is identical for all phases (prototyping, development, deployment, maintenance). There is nothing to redesign at deployment time.
		I want to avoid the "prototyping death spiral" (a lot of fixing and redeployment cycles after delivery to get them right).	There are two problems with the "prototyping death spiral." One is human, and even ZZZZZ cannot address that. But ZZZZZ does eliminate the time wasting and tedious aspects of coding and database maintenance. Because these delaying factors disappear, interactive prototyping becomes not only less painful, it may actually help in refining the application.
Investigative	• What is the size of your application backlog? How many man-years of work is on-hold?		

Here is an example of field marketing messages mapped to both the sales phase and to one genotype. Notice that in most (but not all) phases there are several distinct activities.

First, there is the **opening message** – what a specific buyer genotype needs to know and believe at that phase of engagement. The goal of the message is to move the prospect towards the next phase. In the initial contact phase this may be text on your website home page that describes the product's value and basic features and thus satisfies the prospect that you are worth further consideration, or it could be your elevator pitch spoken at a cocktail party.

Next is the **argument** process. The prospect will have arguments against your opening message. You need to anticipate these arguments and record new arguments as your sales team encounters them. For each argument, devise one or more **responses** to those arguments. Again the goal is to nudge the prospect on to the next phase by removing their resistance.

The last action in a sales phase is often a set of **investigative questions** designed to gather information you need to *personalize* the opening message in the next phase. For example, asking questions about your prospect's business situation at the end of the initial contact phase allows you to draft an initial solution recital.

Now, for some quick notes on how to implement field market messaging at your company:

Messaging – field message development

- Document the "typical" sales engagement phases from discovery through closing
- Identify which genotype is engaged in each phase
- Determine the motivations for each genotype
- Draft the initial message, arguments, responses and questions that will move each genotype to the next phase
- Test and refine
- Make refinement corporate doctrine

This process requires a close working relationship between sales and marketing, which is often a violent and bloody relationship, but one you must force.

Be sure to clearly **document** the sales phases, messages, arguments, responses and investigative questions. Too many people try to do this on the fly or leave it in their skulls. But if five sales people are using five different approaches, or if successes and failures of the draft messages are not recorded and refined, then your sales efforts will flail and fail.

Identify the **genotypes** and in which phases they are involved. Not all genotypes are involved in all phases. Take a product like SAP. IT server administrators are involved but never in the early phases. They are brought in midway as a technical sanity check and again at the end to assure that budgeting for implementation is right. No need to generate a stack of messages for early phases — like the initial contact phase — in which they will not be involved. Great sales people control when certain genotypes are *allowed* to be involved to avoid slowing sales phases unnecessarily.

You should already have itemized motivations for each genotype. Use genotype motivations in creating your field messages and assure that the right motivations are applied at the right phase to the right genotype. Avoid wasting mental bandwidth of one genotype with messages for another — doing so obscures the value propositions and differentiators important to the genotype in question.

Draft messages/arguments/responses/questions and revise them. Then **test** these with a few new prospects and refine again.

Lastly, make **refining** field messages an ongoing work assignment for marketing and sales teams. Sales people will discover what does not work and will often create their own messages for each tiny corner of your field message manual. Make sure that intelligence is captured and used by new sales people going forward, and that marketing sanity-checks the messages for branding and export to mass communications.

I'll repeat one thing again because it is the most important lesson in messaging. *<u>Always</u>* keep the motivations of your genotypes in mind and base your messaging on their expected outcomes. Talking about you is deadly. Talking about what buyers want to achieve is gold. Achieving their expected outcomes, and thus their motivations, is how you create value for them. Articulating that value throughout the communication process is way to stoke their curiosity and keep their interest high as you guide them to an outcome.

Understand that you need to create field messages for non-customers too. Analysts, reporters and investors must receive communications, but they have very different motivations than prospects and customers. It is worth knowing the *stereotypical* motivations of these groups.

Messaging – other audiences

- Always keep the motivations of each audience in mind – they are different
- Lead with the value you deliver to <u>that</u> audience
- Common motivations
  - **Analysts:** Motivated by having a deep understanding of markets, competitors and trends. Educate them so they can educate others
  - **Press:** Telling interesting stories
  - **Investors:** Long-range profitability balanced with risk
  - *None of these genotypes are interested in your sales pitch*

Analysts are in the business of illuminating buy decisions for their customers, which includes your buyers and the media. Their primary motivation is to possess the deepest intelligence about the markets they watch. Your job is to make them smarter. I once pitched to analysts and spent the first half of my presentation not talking about my product, but what we knew about the market that the analyst did not. That earned us a lot of good will, a lot of free ink and the attention of IBM, HP, CA and other partners who saw us mentioned in analyst reports.

Reporters are writers and as such have a singular motivation — to tell an interesting story. Help them tell stories and even write their stories for them. Knowing what their readers find interesting and helping the reporter to *discover* a serviceable angle — in short, doing their job for them — is a good way to get press coverage. Your PR agency should know who writes what in the industry (ink and blogs) and help you orchestrate outreach.

Investors are motivated by money and need to know less about your product and more about your market, profits and prospects for the future. Giving them reasons to invest or not divest is your primary messaging objective.

It is rare, but sometimes, you have to appeal to multiple genotypes with one messaging tool. For example, a new product press release might target reporters and provide them with words that target your prospects. But analysts and investors read those press releases as well, so be sure that no messages in such multi-targeted outreaches conflict or drive away one genotype while taking to another.

Your Action List

1. List to who you will need to communicate, including all genotypes.
2. List when you need to communicate to them and what to communicate.
3. Match motivations against each communication.
4. Create your statement, distill it into a blurb, and then distill your blurb into your elevator pitch, making sure to retain differentiated claims.
5. Map your sales phases, even if they all occur online, and create field marketing messages.

Chapter 8 – Pulling it all together

Now that we have covered some of the elements of strategic marketing, I want to circle back to the beginning and show you why all of this really matters.

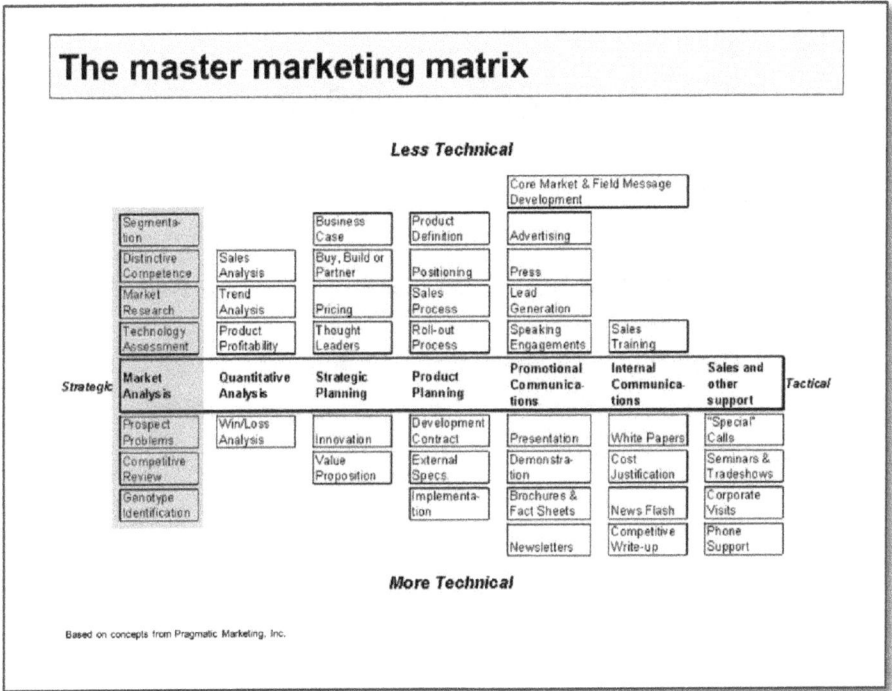

The master marketing matrix

Less Technical

				Core Market & Field Message Development		
Segmentation		Business Case	Product Definition	Advertising		
Distinctive Competence	Sales Analysis	Buy, Build or Partner	Positioning	Press		
Market Research	Trend Analysis	Pricing	Sales Process	Lead Generation		
Technology Assessment	Product Profitability	Thought Leaders	Roll-out Process	Speaking Engagements	Sales Training	
Market Analysis *(Strategic)*	**Quantitative Analysis**	**Strategic Planning**	**Product Planning**	**Promotional Communications**	**Internal Communications**	**Sales and other support** *(Tactical)*
Prospect Problems	Win/Loss Analysis	Innovation	Development Contract	Presentation	White Papers	"Special" Calls
Competitive Review		Value Proposition	External Specs	Demonstration	Cost Justification	Seminars & Tradeshows
Genotype Identification			Implementation	Brochures & Fact Sheets	News Flash	Corporate Visits
				Newsletters	Competitive Write-up	Phone Support

More Technical

Based on concepts from Pragmatic Marketing, Inc.

I showed you this chart early in *title* to illustrate the complexity of formalized marketing. Now I want you to look only at the left-most column, the place where the fundamentals of understanding your market come from. This is where information comes into your organization, information literally shapes your product, your promotional campaigns and your sales messages.

Now imagine doing anything in the other six columns without doing everything the first. How do you build a business case without knowing anything about the business of your key genotypes? How do you write text for a website unless you know what keywords will attract interested customers?

You can't. This is why getting your foundation right is critical. Your house would fall over in the first strong wind if it had a weak foundation. The same applies to your business. Weak foundations make weak products, and in Darwinian economies that makes you an endangered species.

Inbound marketing

- Defined: The acquisition of information to invent/refine products that create value for buyers
- Common research points:
  - **Expected outcomes:** What the buyer expects to achieve
  - **Urgency:** How important is each expected outcome
  - **Gap analysis:** The difference between what is currently offered and the expected outcomes

$$p_{(s)} = 1 - p_{(f)}$$

Thus, the old-school definition of inbound marketing – the gathering of information that is used to pour the foundation of your marketing efforts – is the most important thing you will do. Messages can be edited. Advertising can be reworked. Sales people can be retrained. A bad foundation cannot be easily replaced when a crumbling house is atop it. By the time you discover that your understanding of the market is wrong, *you will have burned through so much cash that recovery is unlikely*. So get your early inbound marketing right the first time.

Remember the old equation for success: The probability of success is equal to one minus the probability of failure. Reduce the probability of failure and you cannot help but succeed.

Within inbound marketing disciplines there are interrelated things you identify that reduce the probability of failure:

Finding **expected outcomes** is the process of learning what customers actually want to *achieve*. This is not a feature, this is a result. CRM systems may have features, but their expected outcome is the coordination of sales and marketing teams for complex sales. Designing a CRM system that does not help achieve that is economically suicidal.

Not all expected outcomes are equal. Some expected outcomes have great **urgency** — people desperately want these outcomes. Other outcomes are less urgent, almost to the point of being meaningless. What is the relative urgency of a sharp scalpel vs. a durable one?

When you know what outcomes people want, then look at the market and see which ones are *not* being met well or at all with existing products (or where your competitors are not properly promoting for the urgent outcomes). This **gap** between expected outcomes and available solutions is where opportunity lies. Any market where most expected outcomes are being met by multiple vendors is a mature and saturated market, and one where new competitors will wither.

Google is a great example. The market wanted to find Web content that was relevant to their inquiries. Search engines that existed before Google returned highly imperfect results, requiring users to scan page after page of returns to find sites that were remotely interesting. The gap was between the expected outcome (relevant content) and existing market solutions (irrelevant results), and the need was urgent because everyone saw great value in rapidly finding the information they desired.

I know I am repeating myself, but the lesson has to be very clear: forget about features. Customers do not care about features. Features are not outcomes. What was the expected outcome from buying an iPod? It wasn't 20-20K flat frequency response with an operating temperature range of 32° to 95°. It was being blindly happy with music. Your features exist only to deliver outcomes. Your features must produce the expected outcomes of your buyer genotypes. Anything else increases the probability of failure.

The subject of inbound marketing gets a bit more complicated when one contemplates accuracy and cost.

Inbound marketing – depth vs. breadth

- ## Too much is as bad as too little
  - –Broad knowledge is good for measuring markets and segments
  - –Deep knowledge is for understanding your target segments
  - –Trying to know everything is fatal — analysis paralysis

First is the dichotomy of the breadth and depth of knowledge. Broad knowledge tells you quantitatively about your market — how big it is, what percentage of the market urgently needs a specific outcome, etc. Deep knowledge illuminates the nuances of your segments or of genotype motivations or competitive threats. You cannot at one instant gather both breadth and depth of knowledge. It is the difference between mass market surveys and focus groups, and there has never been a mass market focus group (you can't fit that many people in a room).

This is one of the many reasons to segment and prioritize your segments. It is better to know much about one segment and the buyers therein than a little about the market as a whole. Since buyers, their expected outcomes and the urgency of their needs differ from segment to segment, you need *broad* understanding of your markets and *deep* understanding of your targeted segments. Brain surgeons and dermatologists use very different scalpels and thus are in two different segments. But if you measured market-wide demand for scalpels, the different needs would have escaped your attention.

The big question to ask vis-à-vis inbound marketing is, "How much detail do you need to know at any given point?" You could spend a lifetime and all your capital learning about your market and all the segments therein, and never get a product out the door. Too much knowledge — often created by reaching too broadly — is a serious form of feature creep. You have to stop somewhere. There is no rule, but General Colin Powell said something interesting about his own process. He claims to research until he has a 65% level of understanding, then he goes with his gut. Most of us do the same though we don't articulate it as well.

You cannot know everything about your market or customers, and it is time-consuming and expensive to try. For each area of knowledge, you will need to perform triage and ask yourself if further study would make a difference in being competitive. If not, then drop it. You will be amazed at what falls from your task list when you honestly evaluate the added value of some information.

Here is a case study to explain the difference. As you saw earlier, Telamon sold software that was only meaningful when used as a plug-in to other software products. We studied the market broadly, measuring who had any expected outcomes from a Telamon-like product (i.e., making pagers automatically annoy people) and discovered six major segments. We studied the segments broadly to estimate the opportunities in each, and discovered that we could and should abandon the bottom three candidate segments since they were significantly smaller opportunities than the top three.

We then dove more deeply into the three top segments, documenting as many of the urgent expected outcomes as we could find with a very limited research budget. After examining these segments, we found a subset of outcomes that were highly common in two segments (some of the outcomes were also expected in the third, but that was irrelevant at that point).

Once we found that two segments had relatively homogeneous expected outcomes, we dove deeply into those two searching for expected outcomes vis-à-vis the software application into which Telamon would plug. We had to make sure we understood what the customers outcomes wanted from the combined operation.

Out of 18+ possible opportunities, we whittled it down to six and initially only engineered four. But that strategy drove revenues 26%+ higher each year, eliminated two competitors, drove another two into the lousy segments we rejected, and made us the de facto solution for HP, IBM and CA customers. Not too shabby. But notice how we swept the data field, broadly first as part of segmenting, and deeply once candidate segments were identified. This is how to work the trade-off between knowing enough and not missing critical information.

Inbound marketing – Telamon case study

- Six major segments
  - Took the top three due to rapidly diminishing opportunity in the bottom three
- Three major partners in each segment
  - Together they controlled 68% or more of their segments
- Prioritized two related segments
  - Similarities allowed bridging two segments
  - Deep study of desired outcomes of partner customers
- Summarized, the approach was
  - Studied broadly to understand and eliminate
  - Prioritized opportunities
  - Studied deeply the top opportunities

Numbers are the easy part of inbound marketing. Buy data from IDC or float a survey and you will collect a series of numbers that keep you from making dreadful mistakes. But this simply shows you where in a specific field of competition you stand against other vendors or against the status quo. To compete requires understanding what the market *desires*, and this is not a **quantitative** measure.

Qualitative analysis involves drilling deeply into the expected outcomes of buyers – their hopes, dreams, fears. It involves helping them discover ***what*** they want to achieve, not ***how*** to achieve it. Too many entrepreneurs are wed to their vision of a product and its features. Buyers do not care about your features. They care about achieving something. You engineer features that help them achieve *their* desired outcomes, not your product vision. Even Steve Jobs studied what people wanted, not what he wanted to give them.

Inbound marketing – qualitative

- Deeper drilling into the hopes, desires, and functional needs of buyers
- Requires buyers to explain what they want to gain (may not be a *functional* result)
- Methods
  - Deep interviews
  - Focus groups
  - Group-think (social network interaction)

There is art in helping people discover their *actual* expected outcomes because they may already have their own perceived feature set in mind, or they may not be entirely aware of what they want to achieve. A prospect might say, "I have to catch a 6 PM flight to New York next Friday." However, if you ask him what he is trying to achieve it might be that he wants to visit his aunt for her birthday. You might have a better way of meeting that objective, like flying him and his aunt to a vacation resort as a birthday gift. Always ask customers where they are going and why they want to go, not how they want to get there.

There are several methods for exploring customer expected outcomes, and none of them are quantitative. **Deep interviews** are conducted by experts who know how to guide conversations toward exposing goals and objectives — of mapping the person's or organization's desired destinations. By comparing and contrasting many deep interviews and finding common expected outcomes, you will identify those outcomes that set the direction for your product features.

Focus groups are like group deep interviews with peer-level reinforcement. Focus groups are best for identifying attitudes and belief systems as they relate to a product, and seeing where peers will influence the decisions of others. The benefit of focus groups is that a group of people can spark large-scale agreements and show urgent outcomes, but they can also create false positives of the same variety. They can also create and deliver a customer-centric vocabulary that describes their motivations, which in turn makes your mass market communications resonate.

Wherever you can find target buyers communing is a potential source for "wisdom of the crowds" research. Online social networks are becoming usable hunting grounds for such things and, for the right researcher, are a cheap way of performing limited or ad hoc focus groups. The problem with social networks is that they are unguided. Finding the answer you need may not be possible and many groups hate nosey vendor intruders. It pays to pay people for their time because this allows you to guide the discussion to your expected outcome, which is to understand their expected outcome.

Quantitative inbound marketing seeks to define the size, scope or momentum of markets, segments, buyers, revenues and competitors, as well as prioritize buyer expected outcomes. By its nature quantitative inbound marketing deals with narrow issues that describe the competitive landscape and very little about what might allow you succeed therein.

There is a place for quantitative analysis for product design. Once your qualitative research tells you what capabilities to create — in order to meet customer's expected outcomes — you can measure and quantify the demand for those features. This is the measure of **urgency**. If there are ten identified features that you could engineer, but budget and time-to-market limit you to doing five, quantitative research will expose the expected outcomes that are most meaningful and urgent market-wide or segment-wide.

Inbound marketing – quantitative

- ## Broad view of the entire market or segment
- ## Primarily a demand or intent measurement
- ## Methods
  - ### Primary surveys
  - ### Analyst surveys
  - ### Customer feedback (mainly negative scorecards)

There are many different ways of doing quantitative research. Surveying is still the best method for original, raw numeric research, which explains all those invitations to participate in surveys littering your email inbox. The Internet has made surveying faster, cheaper and in some ways more reliable. However, two problems have arisen from Internet surveying: First, people have lost interest because there are too many invitations for too many surveys, and you have to incentivize (a.k.a. bribe) people to take your survey. But ease of surveying has also brought a lot of amateur market researchers into the field, and they produce inaccurate results. Surveying is a science and best left to trained and experienced experts who understand survey design techniques and analysis.

Analysts do surveys, and often they have reasonably usable data for sale. However, data that analysts provide may not answer your exact questions, especially if your qualitative research has identified unmet expected outcomes that analyst have not studied. The usability of analyst reports improves as your questions about the market become broader and more generic, or if your questions center on competitor offerings (analysts tend to survey the known market, and thus known competitors). A competent market researcher can deliver more exacting results than a generic analyst study.

Customer feedback can be a good source of quantifiable information if you are consistent in your approach to polling customers, and if you motivate everyone including happy, unhappy and indifferent customers to respond. Many companies only listen to the happy or unhappy customers. Such limited listening causes many marketing mistakes. Listening to just unhappy customers allows you to fix product mistakes but doesn't tell you what delights your current customers and thus what you should strongly promote. Listening to just happy customers helps promote your products but hides potentially deadly defects that your competitors will exploit.

Most interesting is the silent majority. They are neither grossly dissatisfied nor ecstatic with your products. The danger is that indifference allows them to be charmed by competitors. You need to pry into these buyers' brains and discover what would change them from indifferent to evangelical. There is always something that could excite them though they may not know what it is themselves. When turned from being indifferent to happily involved, they will become your unpaid sales force and buzz marketing team.

Sales people hate when I say this, but it is true and must be said. Cut sales out of the customer feedback loop except to find specific information about known issues. Sales folk have a "one fiscal quarter" perspective. Their most recently lost sale, in their minds, stands for everything wrong with your product and they will make that one issue the most urgent for you and your engineering team to solve. This is dangerous except when all the sales people repeat the same thing for an extended period of time.

Sales people are tactically focused, and largely unable to take the long view. Your job — as an executive — is to take the long view. Thus sales feedback has value, but it lacks *strategic* value. Incorporate sales staff feedback mainly in competitive reviews. Sales people will tell you — endlessly — why sales are won or lost, and this typically either informs you about where your product succeeds or fails against competing solutions (or it says something about your organization's ability to articulate your value proposition). It tells you nothing about how to dominate your current segment, what segment to target next or what to engineer in order to invade the next segment.

Inbound marketing – a warning about sales

- ## Sales people are a 3rd tier source for inbound marketing
  - Sales people are not strategically focused
  - Sales people have a one fiscal quarter horizon
  - Sales people think the last lost sale is the reason for all woes
- ## Incorporate their feedback as a <u>small</u> part of your overall inbound intelligence

---

Here is the part you won't like about inbound marketing.

Inbound marketing is complicated by the same infernal matrices that we have examined before. Your research work may map every conceivable combination of product, segment and genotype in your portfolio. This is real work and non-trivial. For smaller companies, doing this work in-house is impractical — keeping such researchers on staff year-round is an extravagant cost. Outsourcing is cheaper than a full-time employee, but not inconsiderable. Yet another reason to study broadly, then dive deep on one or a few target segments. This approach won't break the bank and can be completed before the Second Coming. Diligence is important for your targeted segments. Stay focused on the small and achievable portion of your market and the buyers therein.

Epilogue

Let's put a ribbon on this strategic marketing crash course. There was a lot to take in, so let me distill it for you.

- **Your job is to understand how marketing impacts your products and your company**
- **It is not necessary for you to be an expert in marketing**
- **It *is* necessary that you assure your marketing team performs all due diligence and that they do not try to shortchange you**

Your job as an executive is to understand how marketing impacts your your company and your products. You do not need to be a marketing guru, but you do need to understand, at a high level, all marketing strategy functions. You need to know this to ensure your organization is taking the right marketing steps at the right time. Your marketing director may have the duty of executing marketing functions, but you need to be aware of when he is not performing an essential task or taking the wrong approach.

For start-ups, it is critical to show a grasp of marketing to angel investors and venture capitalists. They already understand marketing and can spot when you don't. Showing them a lack of marketing moxie may squash the desire to trust you with a few million dollars of their money.

There are only two things important to your business: innovation and marketing. Everything else is administrative work. Inbound marketing feeds the innovation engine and outbound marketing promotes your innovations. Marketing is more important than engineering because it defines the products that engineering creates and then gets people to buy those products. Engineering without marketing creates products that nobody wants, or creates products that the market might want but never discovers and thus never buys.

Make marketing a larger part of your job because strategic marketing is not a single event — it is an ongoing process. Schedule quarterly reviews with your marketing staff and product managers to assure they are routinely performing all the functions we have discussed as your market changes (and your market *will* change). Force them to plan and prioritize segment-by-segment dominance strategies.

One question you may have is when to outsource strategic marketing functions. The answer is that you outsource for the same reasons anyone does — to meet a goal without significant risk. Hiring full-time people is expensive and thus creates risk by draining resources.

One rule is that if the marketing task does not require an in-house expert most of the time, then it is better, cheaper and faster to outsource. You should develop in-house competencies when you have grown to the point where you are managing multiple products, are in multiple segments or both. HP, IBM, Apple are all marketing organizations that happen to sell technology. Most start-ups are technology companies that need to market. HP has huge in-house staffs because marketing is a core competency for them. You are not at that point ... yet.

For start-ups and mid-sized companies, most of their marketing strategy work is not core and thus it is often outsourced. With fewer strategic decisions to make on few products and in few markets, outsourcing becomes the preferred alternative to in-house strategy development.

When to outsource marketing

- ## The rule for *all* outsourcing
  - Short-term projects on which you do not need to develop core competency
  - Projects where you cannot afford full-time employees with core competencies
- ## In your early days you face the tough problem of
  - Few in-house core marketing competencies
  - Fewer marketing dollars
- ## Determine which strategic marketing tasks *must* proceed and commit to those first

---

Your job is to determine which strategic marketing tasks need to be performed, how often they need to be done given your market mix and the maturity of your markets, and when the cost of bringing in full-time help becomes less than outsourcing. Sometimes it is not wise to in-source. Silicon Strategies Marketing makes good money on billion-dollar, multi-national corporations who need help with specific projects for specific products, often because they are new products/markets, or the need for strategy is urgent and the hiring process is long.

Your education should not end today. For every two books you read on executive management or technology development, read one on marketing.

There are many books on marketing, and most are not worth reading. However, some shine through the cloudy mess of literature and become classics in the industry. These are books that I personally have read, benefitted from and highly recommend.

Chasm: The Chasm Group books are essential to technology marketing and are required reading. Of these books, *Crossing the Chasm* and *Inside the Tornado* are the two most important because they detail the two most traumatic periods in a tech company's life — when they struggle to get a product into mainstream acceptance and when the market and competitors start to rush them.

Marketing High Tech: Written by an Intel marketing exec, this book is important for many mechanical aspects of technology marketing.

Paranoid: Andy Grove's book — *Only the Paranoid Survive* — is an important read because it discusses critical competitive mapping tactics. Competitors are like sharks — they are all around, they are always hungry, and you are lunch.

New Brand World: In the world of branding, Scott Bedbury cannot be bested. Having defined and managed the Nike and Starbucks brands, he offers the best insights into locating, articulating and evangelizing your brand.

Liars: Anything Seth Goodin writes is worth reading. *Purple Cows, Meatball Sundaes, Idea Viruses* … Seth always has a unique way of illustrating points. However, *All Marketers are Liars* is classic in that he explains a central truth about how people come to accept anything from political promises to shampoo. This one gem is worth the read.

But never hesitate to call an expert. Markets move fast, competitors are swift, and innovations are constant. When getting it right is important, getting the right help is critical. It is your company, don't squander your opportunity by doing everything yourself.

About the Author

Guy Smith is Silicon Strategies Marketing's chief strategy consultant. Guy builds trust throughout your operation via precise marketing guidance and team processes that create buy-in on your marketing strategy.

Guy has earned the trust of many CEOs, founders and marketing VPs in companies around the globe. Guy has led marketing teams and helped executives build consensus within their marketing staffs. A partial list of client companies includes notable firms including Emerson, SUSE Linux, Novell, LogMeIn, LANDesk, DeviceAnywhere, VA Software and others.

Having led, managed and grown his own marketing departments, Guy understands the need for building consensus and establishing buy-in. Guy helps executives build teams ready to implement go-to-market strategies by including key team members in structured strategy development processes. This creates deep confidence in the plan, the team's ability to execute, and the executives who will lead them. Combined, these factors help executives accelerate their company's growth and market dominance.

This unique combination of hands-on technology implementation and technology marketing savvy gives Guy intimate insights into market dominance strategy development.

www.ingramcontent.com/pod-product-compliance
Lightning Source LLC
Chambersburg PA
CBHW032006190326
41520CB00007B/369